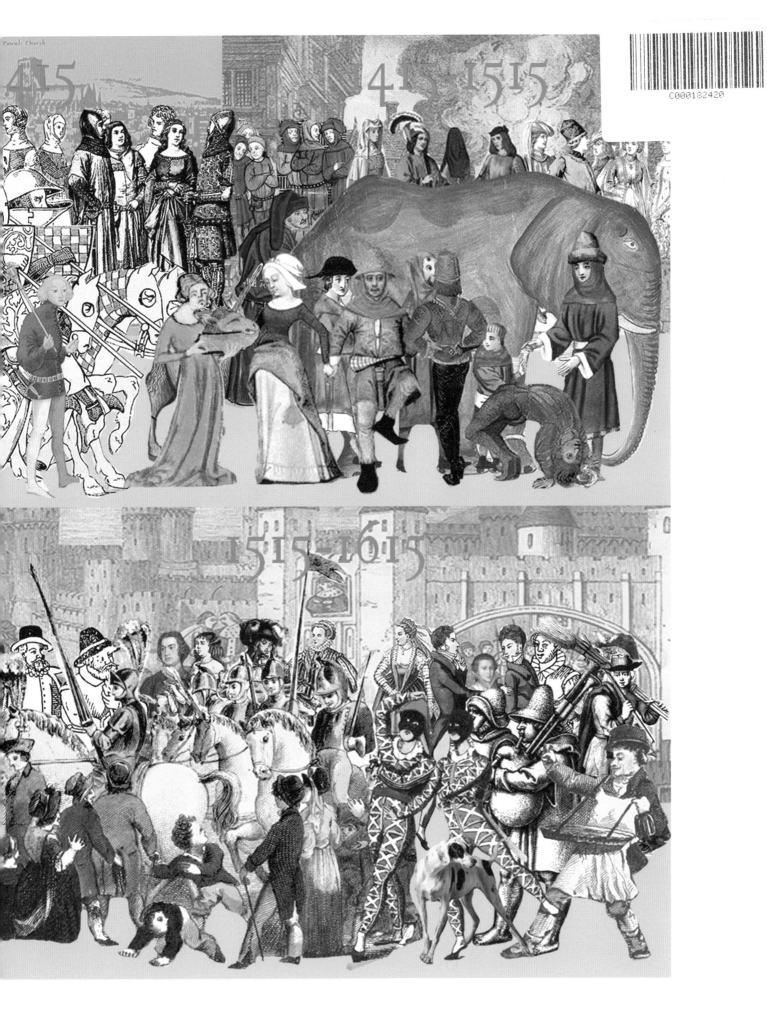

· LORD MAYOR'S SHOW ·

800 YEARS 1215-2015

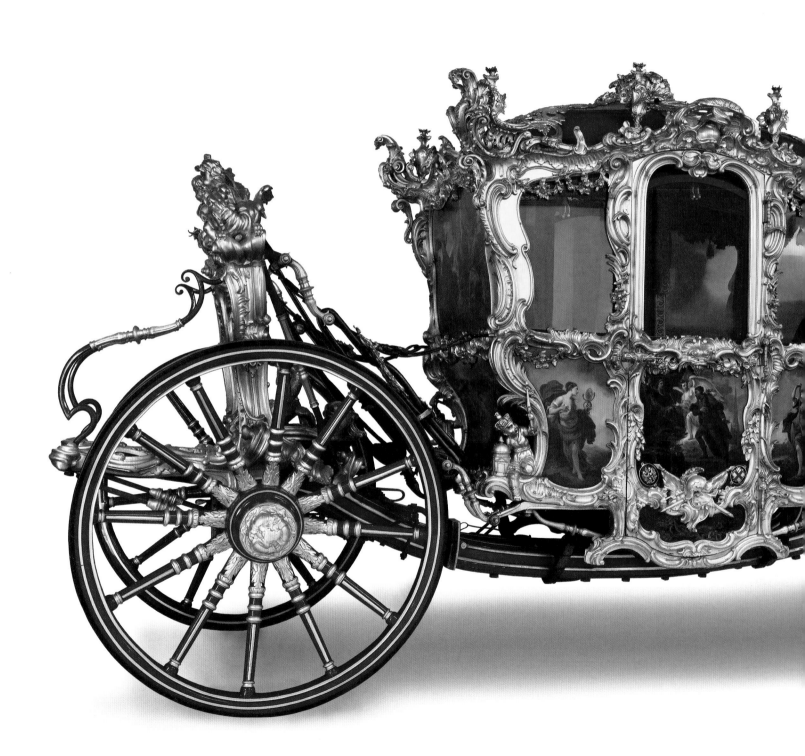

MAYOR'S SHOW •

800 YEARS 1215-2015

Foreword by HRH The Princess Royal

Introduction by Melvyn Bragg

General Editor Dominic Reid

Edited by Hannah Bowen

Third Millennium
Publishing

· CONTENTS ·

PREVIOUS SPREAD:
The Lord Mayor's State
Coach, built by Joseph
Berry of Holborn in 1757
for £860, and first used
in that year.

· NOTE FROM THE GENERAL EDITOR ·

· DOMINIC REID ·

I FIRST CAME ACROSS THE LORD MAYOR'S Show as a small child, in the pages of John Burningham's book *Humbert*, a gift to me from my grandmother. When I was 11, my father was appointed Pageantmaster and, unbeknown to me, a lifelong involvement with the Show had begun. On his death in 1992 I was asked to assume the stewardship of this wonderful historic event and was appointed Pageantmaster at the age of 30.

The Lord Mayor's Show has marched and frolicked its way through history for 800 years. To mark this great milestone we have published the first book dedicated to the history of the Show, and it is to be hoped that this will be a springboard for fresh scholarship. Its fascinating and knowledgeable authors discuss different aspects of an event so old and

many-layered that it defies easy description. The text is set in Doves Type, recently rescued from the mud of the Thames and reconstituted in digital form. London is manifest throughout this book in every way.

As these collected minds have been brought to bear, fresh and welcome definitions of the Show have emerged to add to my assertion that it is above all a platform for good citizenship. The Gentle Author, blogger and publisher, describes the multiplicity of participants and observes 'so many proposals of what it means to be human'. And Melvyn Bragg nails it with characteristic panache by telling us that 'there is splendour and there is a knees-up'.

There certainly is. There has been for 800 years!

DOMINIC REID OBE
Pageantmaster
May 2015

BUCKINGHAM PALACE

For eight hundred years, the Lord Mayor's Show has delighted the crowds of people who come to watch it, as the Procession takes the new Lord Mayor to fulfil their constitutional duty to swear allegiance to the Sovereign each November.

The significance of the 800th anniversary is not just that this unique event has survived those things that might have brought its long and extraordinary history to a halt, but that it has continued to grow in popularity and has found a place of affection, not only in the hearts of Londoners, but in the hearts of the many others who come to watch it and those who, since 1937, have enjoyed it on television.

The Show combines ancient tradition and meaningful ceremony, whilst providing a showcase for much admirable and worthwhile activity. It encompasses the Armed Forces of the Crown, the institutions of the City of London and the good work of many charities and volunteers.

Until now, there has been no book on this rich and varied subject and I am pleased to see this omission rectified. I have a strong connection with the City of London and its Livery Companies; indeed, I participated in the 1992 Show as Master Loriner, so I am delighted to introduce this book to you.

Anne

· A SHORT HISTORY OF THE LORD MAYOR'S SHOW ·

· MELVYN BRAGG ·

THE LORD MAYOR'S SHOW IS A PAGEANT, a carnival of history, and a demonstration of the enduring strengths and spectacular achievements of what Pope Gregory called, in the 5th century, 'a small island on the uttermost edge of the known world.' London has been the capital of that island since the time of Gregory and long before. In its layers of civilization, destruction, creation and survival, it out-Troys seven layers of cities and matches any other city on earth in the deep wellsprings of its past.

This Show, 800 years old this year, is a testament to the tenacity of its subject. Neither the Great Fire of London in 1666 nor Hitler's bombs in the Second World War, nor even the Black Death in 1348 stopped it in its tracks. That was the privilege of a national hero, the Duke of Wellington, whose funeral in 1852 so overflowed London with admirers of the victor of Waterloo that there was simply no room for the Lord Mayor's cavalcade! So the history of the nation made way for the saviour of that nation.

This is one of our country's great celebrations of unity. Despite all the mayhem of years, the Lord Mayor's Show says 'Look. We have come through.' The procession is three miles long, a scarcely rivalled statement of an often ferocious past now washed clean by the blood of time. It flows through the City on the second Saturday morning in November with all the serenity of the Thames which has been its great artery for centuries.

Only the supreme moments in the life of a monarch or the relatively recent Remembrance Day memorializing can be compared with this quietly magnificent drama of what we are, what we were, and what we can be again. 'We' here meaning not only Londoners, but also those whose capital city in war and peace it has been for more than two millennia.

These great collective interruptions to our everyday lives have the character of being a fundamental need. There were pagan ritual days as far back as recorded history itself, there were the glorious Olympics in Athens, there are the booted bristling displays of military might in

OPPOSITE: Waiting for the Show in 1982.

BELOW: William Walworth sitting in his bower, in an 1844 reproduction of an illustration from the Fishmongers' *Chrysanaleia* pageant scroll of 1616.

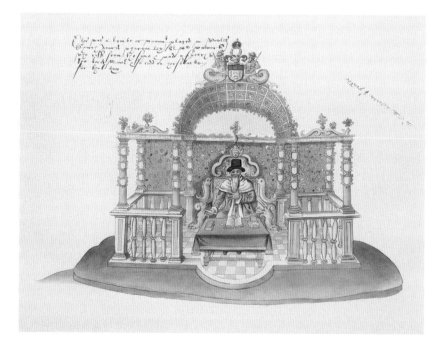

some countries, while in others there is the religiously significant splendour of festivals of the faithful.

There is it seems something embedded in us that needs a great and formal public occasion, so that we can gather together and know that essentially we *are* together. Perhaps it goes back to the first Homo sapiens gathering to look at the sunset and pray for the sunrise. Or perhaps it is an example of what one of London's greatest poets, John Donne, wrote: 'No man is an island...'.

The Lord Mayor's Show enthusiastically embraces the Shakespearean view of life, a particularly English phenomenon founded in literature by the London poet Chaucer, and described by another London author Dickens as 'streaky bacon'. By this he meant that the way we do things here is to put the comic and the tragic against each other; we do coarse and we do grandeur. We do bawdy and we do elegance. In the first two or three hundred years after his death, Shakespeare was heavily criticized by Classicists (especially in France) for this mixture. Well, the Lord Mayor's Show perpetuates it. There is splendour and there is a knees-up.

The 'New Grand State Coach' designed in 1757 by two artists soon to become founding members of the Royal Academy is decorated with panels of high-minded hopes – allegorical figures of Truth, Temperance, Justice and Fortitude.

Then there is the mounted band of the Household Cavalry Regiment in their gold state coats which are otherwise reserved for processions which include royalty. There are the Pikemen & Musketeers, the

BELOW: This aquatint from 1805 shows the Lord Mayor's State Coach during the period when it had a blue roof with a central ornament of 'four boys supporting baskets of fruit and flowers'. The colour of the roof has changed many times.

RIGHT: Yeoman Warders
in undress uniform with
partisans escort the Late
Lord Mayor.

RIGHT: Yeoman Warders
in undress uniform with
partisans escort the Late
Lord Mayor.

Honourable Artillery Company, bands, soldiers, forces of the rich, forces of war, and then the 'floats'. The word itself originated with the Show from the time when its route was on the Thames.

Alongside these glittering arrays there is the other bit of Dickens' streaky bacon. Steel band music, jazz, carnival floats for all, and in one year – 1876 – there were 13 imperial elephants who got more applause than anyone else. And now there is a charitable strand in these celebrations, increasingly geared to the encouragement of young people who need assistance for a lift-up into a world which can be too high a wall for them to climb without help.

Sometimes the high dips into the low with ease. 'Turn again Whittington, Lord Mayor of London' comes from the (fictional) career of a young man who walked up to London where he'd been told that the streets were paved with gold. He failed to make his mark and set off back home, but when he reached the top of Highgate Hill and looked across six miles to the City of London, the bells from the hundred churches of the City rang out to him: 'Turn again Whittington, Lord Mayor of London' – which he was, on three occasions. He became a beloved cultural figure and is still to be seen in Christmas pantomimes around the country with his cat and the bells of the City of London.

In 1381 there was rebellion miscalled 'The Peasants' Revolt' (the leaders were Aldermen, artisans, yeomen and priests). At Smithfield the leader of the rebels, Wat Tyler, was assassinated by William Walworth, Lord Mayor of London, who was then knighted on the field by the 14-year-old King Richard II. This act undoubtedly stopped what could have been the most sweeping

ABOVE: Crowds watching the procession as it passes through Trafalgar Square on 9 November 1918.

rebellion in European history 400 years before the French Revolution. Walworth is still commemorated by the City, especially by his guild, the Fishmongers.

There was the Recruiting Show of 1915 when men fell in behind the procession to sign up. The last time the Lord Mayor rode a horse was in 1711, when he was unseated from his mount by, it is recorded, a drunken barmaid. He broke his leg. Lord Mayors are now confined to coaches.

For ceremonial buffs the Show is an Aladdin's cave. We have the aforementioned State Coach drawn by six horses, the Sword of State, the Great Mace, the cap of maintenance and the wonderful sartorial excesses of the uniforms, not least the Lord Mayor's robes.

The route from Mansion House to the Royal Courts of Justice with only one stopover at St Paul's Cathedral has been modified since the early days when it went in barges up the Thames to pay allegiance to the king at Westminster, or later sauntered down the Strand, then a country lane. Now it has been sensibly curtailed. To get to Westminster would take most of a day! The destination is now the Royal Courts of Justice, which is as it should be since the procession itself came from one of the great documents of our law. The purpose of the procession is for the Lord Mayor to swear his or her allegiance to the Crown.

It was Bad King John who triggered the event. Some poor rulers after their deaths have their legacies revisited, their reputations cleaned up. Not so Bad King John. He murdered his nephews, robbed his lords, interfered with their ladies, lost battles, lied, dumped his old and close friends when it suited him – he single-handedly managed to unite most of England against him. But he sealed (he did not sign; there's no evidence that he could write) Magna Carta, also 800 years old this year.

This is the keystone of our constitutional law, the ultimate guarantor of the limitations of any ruling authority (king or mob) and the foundation stone of liberties. In that charter, London was granted special liberties. It's a charter still alive in our country but also warmly and widely welcomed elsewhere, especially in the United States of America and all over the Commonwealth including in India, the world's biggest democracy.

To bring the City of London onside in the war King John was having with the Earls and Barons in 1215, he granted it a 'commune', a sworn association of townspeople to be headed by a man with another French appellation – 'mayor'. This mayor had to present himself to the King every year to be approved and to swear an oath of loyalty. Over time the King in Westminster was replaced by the Law Lords.

And so the great Show gets on its way at 11am on a Saturday morning. It goes at the speed of 237.6 feet per minute, according to my friend Dominic Reid, the Pageantmaster. He is about to hold the post for a record 24 years, surpassing the previous record set by his father. The spectacle has been depicted by artists, Canaletto and Hogarth for instance, and by writers such as Samuel Pepys and Ben Jonson. It is written deep into our history as shown in the language. The phrase 'after the Lord Mayor's Show comes the donkey cart' (it has to be said that sometimes there are coarser words used for the donkey cart) has now become a proverb. The donkey cart was the dumping ground for the detritus shovelled up after the Lord Mayor's Show, especially that left behind by the horses.

The tentacles of the Show now stretch around the world. As many people see it on television in one year as saw it on the streets in the whole of the 19th century, and half a million and upwards is the size of the crowd that turns out on the morning of the second Saturday of November, every year.

A pageant, a display, a celebration, an emblem of a nation's history and culture, a seamless cohesion between the past and the present, 800 years old. Quite a show of the wealth of one nation's history.

❧ · A SHORT HISTORY OF THE CITY OF LONDON ·

· JEREMY BLACK ·

LONDON WAS FIRST A CAPITAL UNDER THE Romans, when it was the provincial capital. It became the centre of government anew in the Middle Ages: the monarch focused on Westminster and granted a wide range of privileges to London while restricting its development as an alternative power base. Prior to the Norman Conquest, the City already had its own courts as well as distinctive customs and laws. In the early 11th century, the City gained from the Crown the right to appoint its own Sheriff and Justiciar and, in return for an annual payment, to collect royal revenues. Division into wards, which followed by 1127, offered a strong system of local government. Each ward had a wardmote, or local forum, and was headed by an Alderman from whose rank a mayor was elected. The council, or Court of Aldermen, lent coherence to the City's government. Citizenship became an earned right, given in return for membership of a guild, itself secured either by apprenticeship or by purchase, and then by payment through civic taxation; this citizenship was marked by the taking of the civic oath. In return, economic privileges and legal rights were granted, notably the rights to buy and sell property, to trade, and to enjoy the protection of the courts. From 1319, would-be citizens had to gain the approval of those already practising that trade, and citizenship was dependent upon support from existing trade associations. Those excluded were called 'foreigners', irrespective of their place of birth.

BELOW: *London from Southwark*, before the old St Paul's Cathedral was destroyed by the Great Fire. Artist unknown: Dutch School, 17th century.

The significance of London grew greatly as its economy expanded. As a centre of trade and finance, the City of London dominated first England and then the British Isles, and it survived both the Great Plague of 1665 and the Great Fire of 1666. The former killed about 97,000 people, the latter only five, but much of the great medieval city was lost to the flames, including 373 of the 448 acres within the ancient City walls. Bold plans for a new London laid out on a grid pattern fell victim to existing property rights and the pressure to rebuild rapidly. Sir Christopher Wren's St Paul's Cathedral was the masterpiece of the rebuilding, a rebuilding that left the City considerably more attractive visually.

By 1700, London had more than half a million people – more than all other English towns put together; in 1800, it had more than a million. Although industrial growth in the 19th century focused on the north, London remained the centre of trade and finance and was also an important location for manufacturing. Moreover, London's global importance increased as it was the hub for what became the largest empire in the world. The world city, its streets and public open spaces, were the prime setting for the events of imperial splendour. By 1911, the population of the Greater London area had risen to 7,160,000.

The 20th century was an age of troubled glory, as London survived air assault and adapted to the loss of empire and the consequent relative decline of the country. At the same time, the adaptability of London was shown by the resilience of its financial sector and by the ability to create an effective modern city. One of the remarkable features has been the survival of the ancient City of London Corporation as an independent body within the capital, with the Lord Mayor at its head. The City continues to be run from Guildhall, which still stands on its historic site at the heart of the City. And it maintains its ancient ward structure, its Aldermen, its Court of Common Council, and a unique voting system that reflects the combination of a tiny resident population with an enormous commuter population.

·HERITAGE
&TRADITIONS

Section N°. ONE·

· HENRY FITZ AILWIN AND THE ORIGINS OF THE MAYORALTY ·

· NICHOLAS VINCENT ·

SINCE THE 1190s THE CITY OF LONDON has been led by a 'mayor', in effect a 'headman', appointed, like the *podestàs* of 12th-century Lombardy, to arbitrate disputes within the City's oligarchy. The title 'mayor' had first emerged in the Frankish kingdom several centuries earlier. The family of Charlemagne had been 'mayors' of the palace of the kings of France before themselves usurping the throne in AD 751. After 1154, England came to be ruled by the Plantagenet dynasty, previously hereditary counts of Anjou claiming office as stewards and 'mayors' at the French royal court. Applied to the rule of a city as early as the 1130s, Soissons, in the kingdom of France, was briefly governed by a mayor. Thereafter, Italy and Flanders, both in close touch with the City of London, supplied models for such an appointment. Most immediately, in the 1170s, and apparently as a reward for loyalty during the great rebellion of 1173–4, King Henry II had allowed the men of both La Rochelle and Rouen to be ruled by mayors, in the case of Rouen as an appointment for life.

The first Mayor of London, Henry Fitz Ailwin, was in office by 1194, having perhaps been chosen as early as 1189, at the time of Richard I's departure for crusade. As a representative both of the king and of the City oligarchy, he can be assumed to have played a part in suppressing the City uprising of 1196 led by the demagogue William Fitz Osbert or 'Longbeard'. His name, meaning 'Henry son of Ailwin/Aethelwine', and

the fact that his grandfather bore the name Leofstan, suggest that he may have been of English rather than Norman descent. Leofstan, his grandfather, may be identifiable as Leofstan 'the doomsman' who appears in 1108 as reeve of London. By 1130 the house of Henry's father, Ailwin, was being used as a meeting place for the London hustings court, with another

member of the family, Henry's uncle, Robert son of Leofstan, prominent in the London weavers' guild. Henry himself can be found in the records from 1164 onwards, dealing in property, married to a woman named Margaret, with four sons, at least one of whom subsequently married into the gentry.

Henry's own social standing can be gauged from his seal, showing a mounted figure (very much a badge of knightly or gentry status), but here carrying a hawk, rather than, as would be expected of a knight, riding armed into battle. He possessed land in Hertfordshire, Kent and Surrey, a country house at Watton-at-Stone, and a substantial property, with frames for stretching cloth, on the north side of Candlewick (now Cannon) Street. The fact that he retained office for 20 years, and that he was succeeded as mayor by a close associate, perhaps his nephew, Roger Fitz Alan, suggests that he was a remarkably effective fixer. In the 1190s, indeed, it was rumoured that Londoners whispered treasonably 'that they would have no king but the mayor'.

ABOVE: Henry Fitz Ailwin in an engraving from 1813. Note the cap of maintenance and the crossed mace and sword featured at the top, all of these being anachronisms imagined by the 19th-century engraver.

THE MAYORAL CHARTER OF 1215 AND
THE CITY'S MAGNA CARTAS OF 1297 & 1300 ·

· NICHOLAS VINCENT ·

AMONGST THE MANY TREASURES STILL IN
the possession of the Lord Mayor and the City of London
Corporation, few approach the historical significance of the City's
royal charters. From King William I to Queen Elizabeth II, these
link the City to national events, perhaps most famously to the
issue and subsequent rewriting of Magna Carta. The settlement
to which King John put his seal at Runnymede in June 1215
was a response to recent rebellion, and in particular to the rebel
seizure of London a month before.

Since the 1190s, in imitation of Italian, northern French and
Flemish models, London had established its rights to a mayor.
The first such officer, Henry son of Ailwin, had served from at
least 1193 until his death in 1212. In the same year, on 11 July
1212, Southwark and the south bank of the Thames had been
swept by a great fire, interpreted in apocalyptic terms as evidence
that King John was a sinner whose realm was summoned to
repentance. At the same time, tensions between king and City
mounted as a result of the king's taxation, and in particular as
a result of the king's wars with France that led to an embargo
upon much of London's foreign trade.

On 9 May 1215, writing from the New Temple just south of the
Strand, King John issued a charter, still perfectly preserved in
the London Metropolitan Archives, granting 'our barons of our
city of London' permission to elect all future mayors, confirming
all of the City's other privileges and liberties. That same evening,
the king made his way upriver from London to Windsor. His
departure was the signal for disturbances within the City.

ABOVE: The Mayoral
Charter of 1215, which
pre-dated Magna Carta
by almost 6 weeks.

A week later, on Sunday 17 May, whilst the Mayor and chief citizens were at Mass, a group of Londoners opened one of the City gates (almost certainly Aldgate), allowing in a rebel army that had decamped from Northampton. In the ensuing disturbances, not only did the Mayor of London throw in his lot with the rebels, being named as one of the 25 rebel guardians of the settlement agreed at Runnymede, but London came to occupy a leading place in Magna Carta. Clause 13 of Magna Carta guaranteed London's liberties and ancient customs. Clauses 12, 33, 35, 41–2 specifically upheld the rights of foreign merchants and refer to the Londoners' privileges in respect to the payment of taxation, the use of standard measures for wine, ale, corn and cloth and the free navigation of the River Thames. In the civil war that followed, the custody of London remained of crucial significance.

Thereafter, the City's surrender to the Crown in the autumn of 1217 marked the end of hostilities. London's rights continued to be guaranteed in all successive reissues of Magna Carta, not least in 1225 at a time when the City was once again in turmoil as a result of interference by the King's government established in (distinct, and at that time still suburban) Westminster. London almost certainly received copies of the 1215 and 1225 issues of Magna Carta. These, however, have vanished.

Still preserved in the City archives are the original Magna Cartas sent to London by the ministers of King John's grandson, Edward I, in 1297 and 1300. Both are preserved in almost pristine condition. The first still carries its royal seal. The 1297 charter, one of only four surviving originals from this issue, is marked at the bottom with a contemporary address to London, and with a marginal notation ('nota')

ABOVE: The City's letters patent of Edward I (Magna Carta) 1297, which contains a clause confirming the City's rights and privileges.

next to the clauses that continued to uphold the City's privileges, weights and measures. It was accompanied by a letter, still surviving, commanding its publication by the City's Sheriffs. The 1300 charter, one of six surviving exemplars, was recorded in the possession of the City of London Corporation in 1810 but by 1869 was missing. Following its rediscovery a century later in the Public Record Office, it was restored to the Lord Mayor of London by the Master of the Rolls, Lord Evershed, at a banquet held on St George's Day (23 April) 1958.

THE ARCHITECTURAL SETTING·

·DAN CRUICKSHANK·

THE LORD MAYOR'S SHOW IS THE LAST
of the ancient, annual processions through the City of
London. Such processions had, to the medieval mind,
many functions. They were displays of status, prestige
and power, demonstrations of rank, privilege and
allegiances, entertainments, acts of faith, or – like
religious processions through or around churches –

ways of animating architecture through religious
fervour. The Lord Mayor's Show (or 'Triumph', as it
was anciently called) was certainly most of these things.

Its origin lies 800 years ago in the fateful year 1215 when,
just before agreeing the Magna Carta, King John
sought the support of the City in what he feared was

RIGHT: An 18th-
century engraving
showing an exterior
view of Guildhall Yard.

LEFT: A 1653 copy of John Norden's map of the City of London published in his *Speculum Britanniae* in 1593. The coats of arms of the Great Twelve livery companies are displayed in panels on both sides.

a rapidly changing world in which monarchs appeared to be losing some of their grip on absolute power. His ploy was to offer the City a charter allowing it to conduct and control the annual election of its Mayor, and thus bestow upon it a large degree of civic independence and self-government. In return the new Mayor was to present himself before the monarch to 'swear fealty' or feudal loyalty. A deal was acceptable and so was born what is now the oldest continuous municipal democracy in the world.

During the 13th and 14th centuries the election of the Mayor took place on 28 October, the feast day of St Simon and St Jude. This is an interesting choice. In western Christianity the saints are viewed as a pair, evangelizing together in Egypt, Syria, Persia and Lebanon. Both eventually were martyred, and both are said to have been Christ's half-brothers (Mark 6:3 and Matthew 13:55–57). Thus both had a more than usually intimate relationship with Christ and this

evidently appealed to the early organizers of the Mayor's election. The rituals surrounding the initial elections are not known, but in 1378 Aldermen are first recorded as accompanying the Mayor on his journey to make his oath to the monarch, and in 1401 minstrels joined the procession. This would seem to be the moment when the procession started to become a City pageant, with its serious political and sacred intents enshrined within what increasingly became, as Tracey Hill explains, a 'high-profile and very lavish entertainment ... at the centre of the cultural life of the City of London'. It was at this point, in the early 15th century, that the City decided to rebuild its ancient Guildhall, no doubt partly (if not primarily) to play a key role in what had become the City's most important annual festival.

The origin of the Guildhall is lost to us; even its precise and original purpose is uncertain. It is thought that some type of civic hall was constructed in the City in the mid-11th century, during the reign of Edward the Confessor, but the exact role it played in civic life, and whether it was intended to serve a particular guild, is not known. In 1411, when the construction of the existing Guildhall began, its function was clear and its architectural aspirations astonishing. It was the administrative centre of the City, the meeting place of various City 'courts' and it was to be a setting where the Mayor could entertain in regal style, displaying his dignity and that of the City.

Essentially the building was to be, figuratively and literally, the heart of the City. It probably, although not definitely, stands on the site of the original Guildhall (the existing building incorporates what is almost certainly an earlier vaulted undercroft), and in its location the building is approximately at the physical centre of the City as it was in 1411, if the extramural

development of Cripplegate ward north of the City wall is taken into consideration. And just as the Guildhall is the heart of the City, the Great Hall within the Guildhall is the heart and the glory of the building. This room – with its tiers of windows and stone-cut tracery – is still sensational, despite suffering grievous damage in the 17th and 20th centuries. Its high quality helps to put the Guildhall, and its ambitions, in context. In the early 15th century it was one of the largest and most architecturally glorious Great Halls in England. It was a challenge to Westminster Hall, which Richard II had had rebuilt in the 1390s as a symbol of majesty at the Palace of Westminster, and vied with the Great Hall of the Archbishop of Canterbury's Palace. Both these halls are larger than the Great Hall in the Guildhall – and the hammer-beam roof of Westminster Hall is one of the engineering miracles of its age – but perhaps neither eclipsed it for grandeur or beauty.

One of the keys to the beauty of the Guildhall's Great Hall is its proportion. It fills the entire volume of the Guildhall's main floor and is roughly 46 metres long and 15.2 metres wide, so is 3:1 in proportion. This was a proportion – essentially three cubes in a row – that had particular significance in the Middle Ages, and which offers a clue to the building's more secret meaning.

Six hundred years ago, when the Guildhall was designed, the Bible was used as a model for worldly institutions, and texts describing the proportions and forms of sacred objects were taken as inspiration by Christians and Muslims for the design of churches and mosques. These texts include descriptions of Noah's Ark, the Ark of the Covenant and, most significantly, Solomon's Temple in Jerusalem – a building that it was believed had been designed by God, represented the origin of architectural beauty and enshrined the virtues of divine rule and kingship.

The Temple is described in full but somewhat confusing detail in several biblical texts – notably 1 Chronicles, 2 Chronicles, 1 Kings and Ezekiel – and in 2 Chronicles the text notes that Solomon was 'instructed' when building 'the house of God' that its length was to be 'threescore cubits, and the breadth twenty cubits' (2 Chronicles 3:3). So the House of God within the Temple was triple-square in proportion, 3:1, like the Great Hall at the Guildhall. And the House of God was to have a porch, 'the length of it ... according to the breadth of the house', and 'overlaid ... with pure gold' (2 Chronicles 3:4). The Guildhall also has a large porch nearly as deep as the Great Hall is wide, and this was its greatest architectural ornament, completed in around 1430 to the designs of John Croxtone, the

ABOVE: The Great Hall in Guildhall. This 1808 print, which shows the Great Hall following its restoration after the Great Fire, was a collaboration between Augustus Pugin and Thomas Rowlandson: Pugin was responsible for the architectural details, and Rowlandson drew the people.

master mason responsible for the construction of the Guildhall. The porch is now strangely transformed, being re-fronted in 1789 by the City Surveyor, George Dance the younger, in a charming but ersatz Picturesque Saracenic or Mughal style that was, no doubt, regarded at the time as being both novel and sympathetic to the Gothic of the old building. But originally the porch was topped by an image of Christ in Majesty (which seems to have been destroyed when the Guildhall was largely gutted during the Great Fire of 1666), which could have been a reference to the description in the strange and prophetic Book of Revelation of Christ seated – in majesty and judgement – upon a throne, surrounded by a rainbow.

Another and related clue to the building's meaning is offered by the Merchant Taylor and pioneering antiquarian John Stow. In his *Survey of London*, first published in 1598, Stow offered a story about the origin of London. It was an evidently mythic account, but perhaps accepted by many at the time, which Stow inherited from the highly dubious 12th-century historian Geoffrey of Monmouth. Stow writes that Monmouth 'deduceth the foundation of this famous Citie of London' was in 'emulation of Rome' and had been inspired by 'Gods [and] the Trojan progenie'. In Monmouth's view, 'Brute, lineally descended from the demy god Aeneas, about.... 1,108 [years] before the nativity of Christ, builded this city neare unto the river now called Thames, and named it Troynouant or Trenouant.' So London was the New Troy – like Rome of divine foundation – and Britain was named after Brute or Brutus, the grandson of the Trojan, Aeneas. This account, fanciful as it is, must have greatly appealed to early Londoners for it gave their city ancient pedigree and status and cast it as part of ancient classical civilization. Stow does not seem to have entirely believed this story but justified

its inclusion in his *Survey* by quoting Livy, the 'most famous Hystoriographer of the Romans', who argued that exaggeration of the age of cities is 'pardonable, and hath an especial privilege, by interlacing divine matters with human, to make the first foundation of Cities more honourable, more sacred, and as it were of greater majestie.'

For Stow, London was a sacred city – 'divided from East to West and from North to South', like Jerusalem with its four quarters – with the Guildhall at its centre. And Stow made another interesting analogy. He noted that the City was subdivided into wards, 'even as Rome', with Sheriffs instead of consuls and Aldermen instead of senators. Stow observed that the number of these wards was originally, or in the reign of Henry III at least, '24 in all', but in 1393 they were increased to 25 when the large Farringdon ward was divided in two. In 1550 the number of wards was increased to 26, but it has now returned to 25. The number 24 was, for the medieval Christian mind, highly charged. The Book of Revelation could have been a source for this civic structure. It states that around Christ's throne were 'four and twenty elders sitting' (Revelation 4:2–4). The correspondence is clear. The City Aldermen, each representing a ward, perceived themselves as operating in a divine universe, as supporters or advisors of the Mayor who himself owed 'fealty' to the divinely-appointed monarch. And since the Mayor was also an Alderman, the amendment of 1393 happily perfected the biblical model so that the City's Mayor sat 'in judgement' advised by his 24 Aldermen.

It is perhaps not too far-fetched to suggest that the City's structure of government was inspired by this biblical model, not least because of the circumstantial evidence for biblical guidance in the design of the City's most important civic building, the Guildhall. There is the proportion of the Great Hall, but the Guildhall also contains another more direct and dramatic reference to the creative influence of the Bible, and once again the source is the Book of Revelation. Within the Great Hall are images of the fabulous giants Gog and Magog. The current representations replace the early 18th-century wooden images of the giants that were destroyed in October 1940 when the Guildhall was gutted by fire during the Blitz; these no doubt replaced the medieval images of the giants that had been destroyed in 1666. Gog and Magog have a specific meaning. They appear in the Book of Revelation as Satanic figures, the would-be destroyers of God's people, but who themselves will be destroyed in the final battle between good and evil. As the Bible explains, after a thousand years 'Satan will be released from his prison and shall go out to deceive the nations ... in the four quarters of the earth, Gog and Magog, to gather them together in battle' (Revelation 20:7–8). What are these monsters doing within the Guildhall? Presumably they are, symbolically, imprisoned – like Satan – and kept under control by the divine power of the place. And with Gog and Magog defeated and evil destroyed the Book of Revelation reveals, in most visionary manner, that the 'New Jerusalem', the holy city, 'will come down from God out of heaven' and 'lieth foursquare ... the length ... as large as the breadth....' (Revelation, Chapter 21).

Musings about the early meaning of the Guildhall must remain speculative since virtually all papers and accounts relating to its design and construction have been lost. However, it is possible that in the early 15th century the newly rebuilt Guildhall was viewed as an evocation of the Temple of Solomon at the heart of the City that was, itself, the New Jerusalem. Certainly the form of the City – traditionally known

as the 'Square Mile' – is an almost uncanny echo of the biblical description of the New Jerusalem. And if the Guildhall was intended to be an early 15th-century vision of the 'House of God' in Solomon's Temple, then presumably the Mayor was expected to possess the wisdom of Solomon himself; certainly, like Solomon, he sat in judgement within his 'Temple'.

The Guildhall today is a remarkable fusion of substantial early 15th-century remains and erudite post-Second World War repairs and reconstruction, essentially in the Gothic manner, undertaken by Sir Giles Gilbert Scott. His major addition is the roof to the Great Hall, with its stone arches. Scott is best known for Liverpool's Anglican cathedral, Battersea and Bankside power stations (the latter now serving as Tate Modern), and for his design of the 1926 and 1936 telephone boxes. Yet his sensitive and thoughtful work at the Guildhall is among his finest achievements.

The Guildhall is the location, the day before the Show, of a curious but critical ceremony in which the outgoing Lord Mayor symbolically hands power to his successor. This is done without speeches, so the handover is called the Silent Ceremony. And, ever since the Guildhall was completed, on the day of the Show the new Lord Mayor goes on a journey that takes him or her through the material and immaterial City, from the profane to the sacred and back again. It is also a journey that takes them to, and past, some of the best buildings in Britain.

First, when leaving Guildhall Yard, the Lord Mayor passes Sir Christopher Wren's St Lawrence Jewry. Its fine, temple-like east elevation does much to suggest that the Yard is synonymous with the court that the Bible states stood in front of the 'House of God'. And, as with other City churches along the way, the

bells are rung, like temple bells, in celebration and to sanctify the air.

The Lord Mayor then passes the Bank of England (a building situated on the route only since the expansion of the Bank in the 18th century) and arrives at the eastern end of Poultry, where the Stocks Market was located in medieval times. This junction of major roads and buildings, including the Bank and the Royal Exchange, became the financial centre of the City, and, in a sense, the heart of empire. Here, on the site of the

Stocks Market, used for the sale of fish and flesh, was erected from 1738 to 1751 one of the most remarkable buildings in Britain. It is a veritable palace – great, grand and dignified – created by the City to serve as the official residence and office of its Lord Mayor. Mansion House, as this palace is called, is not nearly as well known – or appreciated – as it deserves to be. This is partly because its spectacular interior is not generally open to the public, partly because the site on which it stands is cramped with traffic thundering close to its noble porticoed north elevation and partly

BELOW: The Lord Mayor's State Coach in Guildhall Yard on Lord Mayor's Day; St Lawrence Jewry can be seen to the right.

because it received a poor reception when completed. London's mid-18th century arbiters of taste believed that nothing fashionable or truly elegant could emerge from the solid, commercial and mercantile world of the City, and when Mansion House was revealed to the world, fault was found: it was not just criticized, but, crueller still, the building and its clients were mocked. The third edition of James Ralph's *A Critical Review of the Public Buildings, Statues and Ornaments in and about London and Westminster*, published in 1783, states that Lord Burlington, the great champion of Palladian architecture that became the aristocratic fashion of early 18th-century Britain, submitted a drawing by Palladio to the City when the design of Mansion House was being considered. Palladio had been dead for over 150 years, but, states the *Critical Review*, 'great debates ensued' in the Common Council as to whether the said Mr Palladio 'was a freeman of the city or no'. The discussion only stopped when it was discovered that Palladio 'was a papist', and thus ineligible. Instead, 'the plan of a freeman and a protestant' was adopted. The successful plan had been produced by George Dance the elder, the City's own surveyor. The usurpation of Palladio or of a Burlington-approved neo-Palladian architect by a humble City surveyor for such an important project seems to have caused deep affront. Years later, in 1744, when Dance's building was nearing completion, Burlington was asked his opinion about carving for the main pediment. He refused to involve himself, and is reported to have commented that 'anyone would ... carve well enough, for that Building'.

This early criticism is unjust. Mansion House has an ingenious plan and some of the best interiors of their date in London. Some of these are in the Palladian manner – because, despite Burlington's disparaging

LEFT: Sir Thomas Gresham founded the Royal Exchange in 1566. The golden weathervane on top of the building takes the form of his family's emblem, the grasshopper.

BELOW: A view of Mansion House showing the attics and the Lord Mayor's State Coach passing by, based on a drawing of c.1757–60.

LEFT: *Cheapside 10.10 a.m.,*
10 February 1970 by Ken Howard.

On the day of the Show Mansion House is a gathering place for the Lord Mayor's guests who can watch the parade from a temporary grandstand erected in front of the portico.

During the Show the Lord Mayor, ensconced in his magnificent State Coach, heads west from Mansion House, along Poultry and Cheapside, which together form, by tradition, the main commercial artery of the City. Cheapside (originally known as Westcheap) was the location of luxury shops, inns, markets, mansions, mercers' premises and, from the mid-14th century until the 18th century, of goldsmiths and jewellers who had their own 'quarter' at the west end of the street. This part of the progress is, for the Lord Mayor, very much a ride through the material world.

At the west end of Cheapside is St Paul's Cathedral. Built between 1675 and 1711, the cathedral is the masterpiece of Sir Christopher Wren and his band of inspired and able craftsmen and assistants – including Nicholas Hawksmoor and Grinling Gibbons – and is without doubt one of the greatest churches in the world. Here the more sacred aspect of the procession, and of the Lord Mayor's office, is emphasized. The Lord Mayor and his or her consort stop outside the cathedral, and, with Wren's architecture as a magnificent backdrop, the Dean blesses the Lord Mayor and the mayoral office. Interestingly, as if to act as a subtle reminder of the role biblical texts have played in the life and look of the City, an image of Christ seated on a rainbow can be seen in the choir of St Paul's Cathedral. The image, rendered in mosaic, was not installed until the late 19th century; nevertheless, designed by Sir William Blake Richmond, it is strangely pertinent to the pageant.

attitude, Dance's design is grandly Palladian – and some in the lighter Rococo style, with graceful *rocaille* ornament. The most magnificent interiors are the ballroom and the banqueting room, the latter inspired by Palladio's design for an 'Egyptian Hall', and both were fitted with lofty attics that, seen from outside, loomed high above the main body of the building. The cubical Egyptian Hall – originally with a ceiling twice as high as the width between the room's impressive internal colonnades – was no doubt yet another attempt to recreate the 'House of God' or Holy of Holies from Solomon's Temple, this time probably under the influence of Freemasonry. (Dance was a Mason and Master of the Bell Tavern lodge in Nicholas Lane, Lombard Street.) Sadly, the strange attic superstructures – nicknamed the 'Mayor's Nest' and 'Noah's Ark' by amused Londoners – were both later removed to give the building a more conventional and seemly silhouette.

The Lord Mayor then progresses west along Ludgate Hill and Fleet Street to the Royal Courts of Justice. En route images of Gog and Magog appear again, this time as part of a clock of 1671 located outside the church of St Dunstan-in-the-West on Fleet Street. Quite why the giants appear here, chiming the hours, nobody knows. At the courts, the most important constitutional part of the Show takes place when, before the gathered justices, the Lord Mayor swears allegiance – 'fealty' – to the monarch, and so fulfils the promise made to King John 800 years ago.

As it happens, the setting in which this medieval vow is honoured is utterly appropriate. The courts were begun in 1874 to the design of George Edmund Street, and, although a complex modern building in which multiple uses mix in discrete and exclusive manner, and where services are integrated most cunningly with the architecture, it is also one of finest pieces of fairy-tale neo-Gothic in London. It is a building of many faces. Its frontage on the junction with Fleet Street and the Strand, near the site of Temple Bar and so on the boundary between the cities of London and Westminster, is a most erudite composition. Street wanted to create a great modern public building in the true spirit of late 13th-century English Gothic, the style that was most admired from the mid-19th century as the perfect form of medieval Gothic. The frontage is marvellously and picturesquely asymmetrical in the authentic Gothic manner, with the exterior design reflecting the logic of interior arrangements. There are squat towers – a pair forming a gatehouse – with pointed or pyramid roofs that help give the building a deliciously romantic silhouette, a Gothic arcaded walkway that prances along at high level in a mysterious manner and staircase towers fitted with tiers of windows with diagonal cills marking the rise of the staircase within and thus revealing their function.

The main frontages of the building are clad with stone, but subservient side, rear and courtyard elevations are mostly faced with brick, banded with stone, to create an altogether more utilitarian and familiar 19th-century feel. These elevations are not without their architectural moments: one courtyard, for example, is distinguished by a fine Venetian Gothic-style arcaded loggia. But the architectural glory of the building is its vast, rib-vaulted and stone-clad Great Hall. Measuring 70 metres in length and 25 in width, it is roughly similar in proportion to, if much larger in scale than, the Great Hall in the Guildhall.

BELOW: Gog and Magog at St Dunstan-in-the-West.

LEFT: An engraving of David Roberts' *St Paul's Cathedral (The Civic Procession, Lord Mayor's Day)*, 1844.

through this lofty and vaulted hall that the Lord Mayor processes to renew the time-honoured oath of their office.

The Lord Mayor's Show is a fantastic affair and the architectural theatre of its setting is superb. It involves or passes by some of the best and most thought-provoking buildings in England, and moves along ancient thoroughfares – Cheapside, Fleet Street, the Strand – that are woven into the very fabric of national memory. Altogether there is, quite simply, no show like it on earth.

This hall – solemn, cavernous and a powerful evocation of the architectural grandeur of the Middle Ages – is a worthy setting for any extreme of chivalric fantasy or ancient ceremony, and so it is most fitting that it is

ABOVE: A woodcut engraving of the new 'Palace of Justice', published by *The Illustrated London News* in 1882, the year in which the Royal Courts of Justice opened.

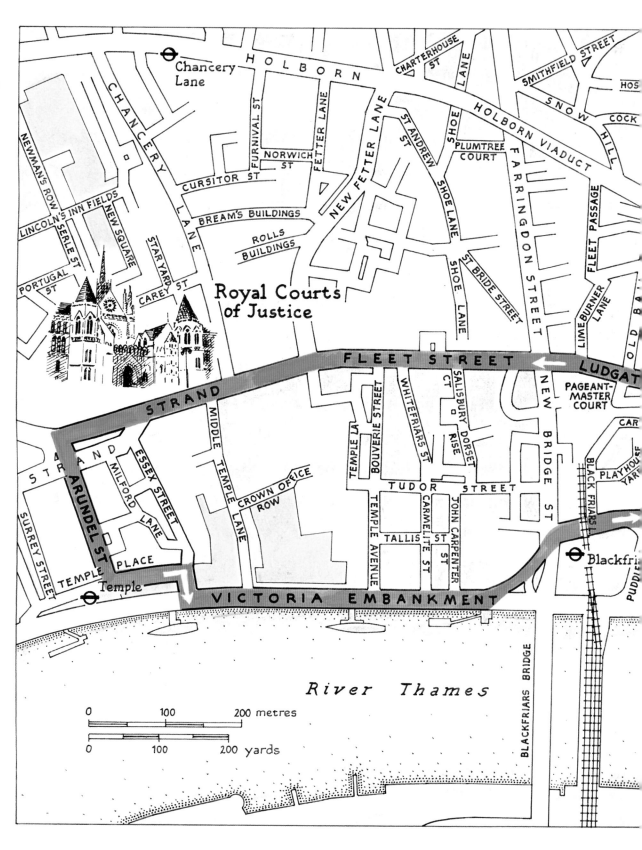

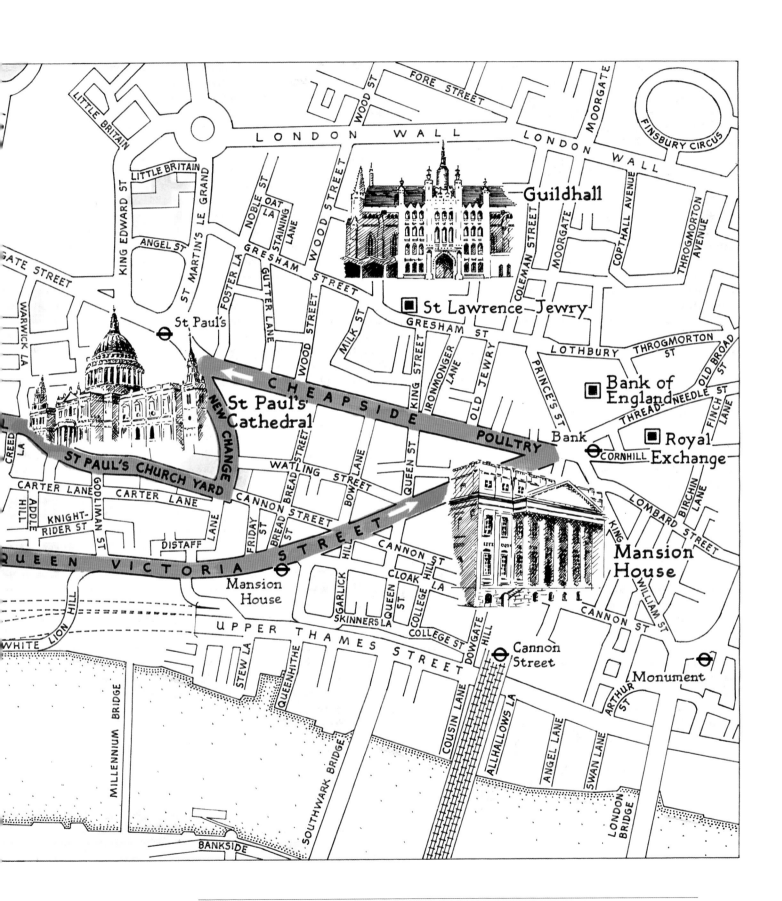

· THE ROLE OF THE PAGEANTMASTER ·

· DOMINIC REID ·

SOME 450 YEARS AGO THE NAMES OF those responsible for creating the Lord Mayor's Show began to appear in the records of the City's livery companies. In 1556 John Leedes was asked to build a 'decent and comely pageant' for Sir Thomas White. And we know that Richard Baker was responsible for the Show in 1566, and that he was succeeded in the role by his son Peter.

These men were poets or artificers. They wrote the script for the pageant or they created its props and costumes. The Show was then spoken like a medieval mystery play, and the role became known as 'City Poet'. There were some famous City Poets including Thomas Dekker, Anthony Munday and Thomas Middleton, and even a failed attempt by Ben Jonson.

The last spoken Lord Mayor's Show was performed in 1702, when Elkanah Settle wrote the Show for the Vintners' Company. Settle was a complex and ultimately unsuccessful character who ended his days performing inside a green leather dragon costume. Alexander Pope put this couplet in his mouth:

Yet lo! in me what authors have to brag on!
Reduced at last to hiss in my own dragon.

The Corporation refused to recognize the title City Poet, and so it fell into disuse.

Today the Pageantmaster is responsible for every aspect of the design and production of the Lord Mayor's Show. This ancient and well-loved celebration is a platform for good citizenship. It is made up of over 150 different elements ranging from dramatic floats, military bands and marching detachments, to horses and carriages and the Lord Mayor's gilded State Coach.

BELOW: Instruction booklets are produced each year for the civic participants and Marshals.

BELOW LEFT: The sign for the street named in John Reid's honour by the City of London in 1992.

PAGEANTMASTER COURT EC4

CITY OF LONDON

Formerly Ludgate Court

ABOVE: Snowdon's 1984 portrait of John Reid.

BELOW RIGHT: The Pageantmaster's hat, sword and gloves.

The participants are drawn from all walks of life and number some 7,000 on the day itself. This temporary community is marshalled into an orderly procession and delivered with split-second accuracy to an audience watching it on the street and live on television. It has been broadcast since 1937, making it the longest running television programme in the world.

A great deal of work goes into the planning process. Modern attitudes to safety, security and risk have made effective liaison with a wide variety of agencies more important than ever. But the job is also an interpretive one. The Ceremonial Handbook of the Corporation of London states:

> Ceremonies are not idle forms or shows, put on merely for entertainment. They ensure that things are done with dignity and in good order. More than this: they embody and make visible rights and privileges ... If however ceremonies are to make their full impact it is vital that the reason why they are performed should be clearly understood. Without such understanding, ceremonial tends to be regarded merely as a traditional form of behaviour or a piece of pageantry.

The job of the Pageantmaster is therefore above all to create a series of elegantly linked ceremonies that are both legible to the onlooker and which confer dignity upon the participant. They must also answer the requirements of the City of London (Various Powers) Act 1959 for the Lord Mayor to swear an oath of loyalty to the sovereign on the second Saturday in November every year.

Ceremonies have a language and a syntax all of their own which are deeply embedded in the national psyche. Any dissonance is easily picked up by the audience who would soon lose interest in something which made no sense. And so the opportunity exists for the Pageantmaster to interpret and craft the procession and each moment surrounding it with a latitude which does not exist elsewhere within state ceremonial. Therein lies the challenge and the excitement of the job.

My father, John Reid, produced 20 Shows between 1972 and 1991 and held the record for tenure in the post of Pageantmaster until this record passed to me in 2012. He was responsible for rescuing the Show from the parlous state into which it had fallen. On his death in 1992 the City saw fit to add to the many rich traditions surrounding the Show by naming a street off Ludgate Hill 'Pageantmaster Court' in recognition of the service he gave to the City. And so, each November the Lord Mayor's Show passes this monument to those who have brought it into being.

· THE LIVERY COMPANIES ·

· DAVID GIBBS ·

AMIDST THE GLEAMING GLASS TOWERS and restless crowds inhabiting the Square Mile are the halls of the City livery companies, institutions that have enriched the life of the City of London since the Middle Ages. Many of these halls are architectural masterpieces in their own right. Skinners' Hall, now overlooked by the monumental Cannon Place, has been on the same site on Dowgate Hill since 1327; Michael Hopkins' striking Haberdashers' Hall in West Smithfield, opened in 2002, is their fourth hall since 1461. Where do these companies and their halls come from? How have they survived rapacious Stuart monarchs, the Great Fire, the Blitz, developers, and the financial shenanigans that have been a recurring feature in the City's history?

Most were founded between the 12th and 15th centuries. Charters were granted by the monarch and with them, monopoly powers. Their names suggest their original purpose – Mercers, Drapers, Merchant Taylors, Grocers, Fishmongers, Ironmongers, as well as Goldsmiths and Vintners. A mixture of trade association and craft guild, they decided who could work or trade in their craft, controlled prices and wages, determined working conditions and welfare, and vigorously ensured quality control: the Bakers, for example, introduced their 'dozen' to prevent the short-changing of customers.

The members of a guild were known as liverymen (denoting the right to wear a particular uniform or livery); they also included freemen and apprentices. Governed by a Master, supported by Wardens and a Court of Assistants, they were self-governing communities, professional, charitable and sociable. Often the livery companies were closely associated with religious fraternities. Members of a company worshipped together. They helped their members (and others) in bad times, cared for orphans, the elderly and sick, acted as burial societies, and fostered the young through apprenticeships.

The richer companies built lavish halls in which they conducted their business and demonstrated their success to the rest of the City. As with many medieval Londoners, they loved ceremonies, pageants and festivals, be it for the installation of a new master – the Skinners to this day still have a police horse escort on the feast of Corpus Christi – or a new Lord Mayor, which in those early days involved a procession on the river up to Westminster, a scene recorded memorably by Canaletto.

Precedence was all-important. In 1484 the Skinners and Merchant Taylors jostled on the river as to who was sixth and who was seventh. That

BELOW: Sir William Ryder, Haberdasher and Lord Mayor of London 1600–1.

Sr Wm Ryder: Haberdasher Lord Mayor of the City of London 1600.

ABOVE: The Livery Hall at Goldsmiths' Hall.

evening the two sets of apprentices, emboldened by strong drink, resorted to fighting in the street and two were killed. The new Lord Mayor, Robert Billesdon, was furious. He summoned the two Masters: 'I will not have this great City brought into disrepute in this way. In future you will alternate on a yearly basis between six and seven and he who is sixth will entertain to dinner the seventh.' The Billesdon Dinner is still, more than 500 years later, the annual highlight of both companies' calendars, reminding everyone that when at 'sixes and sevens' – this incident being the origin of the phrase – a good meal in convivial company often helps to solve the problem.

Economic expansion in Tudor and Stuart times resulted in the decline of the craft guilds and the break-up of monopolies. Some companies became involved in overseas ventures to Ulster, Muscovy and Virginia, or funded searches for the Northwest Passage, whilst the Clothworkers sponsored the greatest geographer of the age, Richard Hakluyt.

The companies have never stood still. Now there are 110 of them, ranging from the Great Twelve (the earliest and largest) to the 33 that have been founded since 1930, including the Management Consultants, Information Technologists and Marketors.

What do livery companies do today? First, and most importantly, they promote, sponsor and lead a variety of charitable and educational activities. Many of these projects are represented in and celebrated by the Lord Mayor's Show each year. For instance, projects supporting the elderly date from the days when many companies ran almshouses. Historically they have run as trusts some of the leading independent schools in the land, including St Paul's (Mercers), Oundle (Grocers), Tonbridge (Skinners), Merchant Taylors' and Haberdashers' schools. Nowadays, they are especially involved in primary and secondary state sector education, sponsor academies such as the City of London Academy, Southwark, and provide outstanding apprenticeship schemes for young people. The founding of the City University in 1966 was driven by several companies; the Salters have played a notable role in developing chemistry education at all levels; whilst the City and Guilds Institute, now with 8,500 centres in more than 100 countries, especially in the developing world, was a joint enterprise between a group of companies and the City of London Corporation.

Second, the companies play an important role in the governance of the Square Mile. All liverymen are freemen of the City, and as part of this responsibility elect the Lord Mayor and the Sheriffs from their number. Third, they provide an opportunity for people from all walks of life to meet in a convivial environment, to discuss and debate the great issues of the day, and to reflect; not unimportant in an age when so many in the City appear to be running faster and faster, consumed by the quest for gold.

THE WORSHIPFUL COMPANY OF PATTENMAKERS ·

· TIM CONNELL ·

PATTENS WERE RATHER LIKE WOODEN slippers, and from medieval times they were used to keep the wearer's shoes and feet out of the mud. They were worn mainly, though not exclusively, by women, hence the Pattenmakers' motto *Recipiunt fœminæ sustentacula nobis* ('Women receive support from us.')

Samuel Pepys writes of his wife having trouble with a new pair, and they are mentioned frequently in novels ranging from *Northanger Abbey* to *Bleak House*. Pattens were in common use until early in the 20th century when improvements to roads and pavements, changes in fashion and the increasing use

ABOVE: A pair of early 19th-century pattens.

OPPOSITE: The Pattenmakers' float in the Lord Mayor's Show in the 1920s.

of rubber for boots made them obsolete. They were inexpensive workaday items, which meant that their makers were fully occupied rather than prosperous. The Pattenmakers' guild was based around the Church of St Margaret Pattens, near the Monument.

The origins of today's Pattenmakers' Company are uncertain. Their first charter dates from 1670, although the earliest mention of the 'Mystery of Patynmakers' dates from 1379 and there are constant references to the guild and its related trades in other sources. In 1607 galoshes with gold buckles were given to Prince Henry, the eldest son of James I. The Company supplied men for the Watch and military service, and took part in the processions which since time immemorial have formed part of life in the City.

The same is true of feasting and even a small company like the Pattenmakers met regularly for the Common Meal. As they had no hall, they would meet in City taverns and the custom developed in the 18th century of adding a procession. In 1790, for example, 30 liverymen processed from the White Hart in Cannon Street and back, via Gracechurch Street, Bishopsgate Street, London Wall, Cheapside and Cornhill. By 1802, when they chose to dine at the White Hart, the procession included musicians who performed twice outside Mansion House. The custom developed of parading on Lord Mayor's Day, possibly at a time when the main procession still took place on the river. Funds had been made available under the will of Thomas Scrimshaw, who died in 1775. He left the significant sum of £1,000, half of which was to 'defray the expenses against all unlawful workers', the other to fund 'a March and a Dinner once in three years on the Lord Mayors Day on the 9th of November for ever'. He added a note that, should the Pattenmakers not accept, or refuse to act, then the whole amount would be given to the Worshipful Company of Curriers. This caused some difficulty in 1818 when the Lord Mayor's Show was cancelled following the death of Princess Charlotte. The Pattenmakers were concerned that they might lose the bequest if they did not parade, but were told firmly by Mansion House that they would not – and should not.

A march clearly predated Scrimshaw's will as there is a reference to Colours being 'much worn' in a report of 1720, which also refers to the march. Since the Company paraded on the day of the Lord Mayor's Show it was perhaps inevitable at some stage that the two parades would clash. It is said that on one occasion the Clerk of the Company, having been ordered to move by the Chamberlain, refused to budge. From this impasse the practice emerged of the Pattenmakers being incorporated into the Lord Mayor's Show every three years, and this (with the exception of the war years) has continued to this day. The Pattenmakers are the 70th Company in order of precedence, and – given City protocol, where juniors lead – every year in the Lord Mayor's Show they proudly appear in front of the Great Twelve, who comprise the most ancient and important livery companies.

· THE ORDER OF ST JOHN ·

· TOM FOAKES ·

IN 1886 THE ST JOHN AMBULANCE
Association carried out its first official 'public duty'
at the Lord Mayor's Show, a year before the official
formation of the St John Ambulance Brigade, which
was established to provide free first aid and medical
care to the public, complementing the free first-aid
training offered by the Association. This relationship
with the Lord Mayor's annual procession through

the City's streets, and with the City itself, has endured
and developed so that St John today is an integral part
of public events in London.

While St John is a charity with a vital modern role in
supporting the teaching and provision of first aid and
medical care, its humanitarian purpose has ancient
origins. The Order of St John maintains its original

BELOW: The St John
Dick Whittington float
in the 1967 Show.

Lord Mayor's Day, 1901.

Scene outside the Royal Courts of Justice.

By kind permission of the proprietors of "THE SPHERE."

headquarters just beyond the City, in St John's Gate, Clerkenwell, the remaining part of a 12th-century priory that occupied the site. However, St John was at first a religious order, founded in the 11th century to care for sick pilgrims in the hospital that it established in the holy city of Jerusalem.

Increasing religious tensions at the end of the 11th century resulted in the declaration of the First Crusade by Pope Urban II in 1095. The Knights Hospitaller, as the Order became known, joined the struggle to retain Jerusalem as a Christian stronghold, although the fall of the city in 1187 led to the Order's slow retreat westwards across the Mediterranean.

The Order travelled first to Acre, in Syria, and from there it withdrew to Cyprus, then Rhodes, and finally to Malta, where the Order arrived in 1530. For the following 250 years the Order fortified and embellished the capital, Valletta, until in 1798 it surrendered to

Napoleon and lost its island stronghold. Briefly seeking refuge in Russia under Tsar Paul I, the Order finally settled in Rome, where it remains today operating as an international humanitarian charity.

The Order in England is a separate and distinct organization revived in the 19th century after its dissolution by Henry VIII in 1540. Seeking a relevant social purpose in a Britain that was dominated by industry but without the benefit of a national health service, founding Order members established St John Ambulance to provide standardized first-aid training to all. Ten years later, in 1887, the St John Ambulance Brigade was founded, the purpose of which was to offer free first aid and medical care to the public on any occasion where crowds gathered.

St John's presence in the Lord Mayor's Show continues to maintain a dual purpose. The annual float is the work of St John volunteers throughout London, who take inspiration from St John's 900-year history to present different themes each year. The French Field Hospital established by St John during the First World War was the focus in 2014, and other years have featured Crusading knights, vintage ambulances, marching bands and representatives from the significant youth groups within St John, the St John Ambulance Badgers and Cadets.

Perhaps of greater significance are the many volunteers who man the first aid stations along the parade route. Each year, hundreds of St John Ambulance volunteers provide first aid to the public, ensuring that all who attend the annual procession are cared for in accordance with the Order's founding Christian principles: 'For the Faith' and 'For the Good of Mankind'.

· CHRIST'S HOSPITAL ·

· JOHN FRANKLIN ·

THE HISTORY OF CHRIST'S HOSPITAL
doesn't quite span 800 years since the Lord Mayor's
Show began, but almost five centuries is still a remarkable
achievement for a school, particularly one that remains
true to its original mission. Christ's Hospital, also referred
to as the Bluecoat School, was founded in 1552 to educate
poor children. The Lord Mayor, Sir Richard Dobbs,
received a letter from Edward VI asking him to address
the needs of the poor, whereupon he quickly gathered
a 'committee of thirty' to raise money to establish the
School. Governors were elected to serve the School and in
November 1552, Christ's Hospital opened its doors to 380
children in the old buildings vacated by the Grey Friars in
Newgate Street. Edward VI became patron and founder
and a Royal Charter was signed to this effect 11 days
before his death in 1553.

The infants amongst the 380 children were sent away
to Hertford to be looked after by nurses and sent
back to London to be educated when they were aged
ten or older. At Newgate Street, the pupil numbers
in just one year grew to over 500. They were provided
with food, clothing, lodging and 'a little learning', and
were not only cared for but prepared for the job market.
Girls were admitted from the beginning but were in the
minority. The School prospered and stayed in the City
for 350 years until a new school was built in Horsham,
West Sussex, to which the boys were transferred in
1902. The girls, who were at the Hertford School,
joined the boys in 1985.

ABOVE: A first day cover of the Royal Mail's 1989 stamp
issue commemorating 800 years of the Mayoralty.

BELOW: Christ's Hospital Band passing St Paul's Cathedral.

Today, Christ's Hospital's links with the City are strong. The Lord Mayor is Vice President and has the ancient right to 'present' six children to the School. It is a great honour for these pupils, who usually meet the Lord Mayor on ceremonial occasions such as Speech Day.

The School's first participation in the Lord Mayor's Show took place on 9 November 1906, when the Head Master, Reverend A.W. Upcott, and three Grecians (Upper Sixth Form pupils) were invited to attend. The band made its first appearance in 1981 and has been invited to participate ever since. The band led the procession in 1989 to mark the 800th anniversary of the Mayoralty, and a special first day cover was produced for the School to mark the occasion.

Old Blues (former pupils) have also held the position of Lord Mayor, the most recent being Sir Richard Nichols in 1997. This special year was celebrated with the creation of a bus and Tube poster, featuring a Bluecoat boy as drum major, used on the front cover of the Show programme. Christ's Hospital also entered a float into the procession that year: because of Nichols' association with the Salters' Company, and to recognize the support the Salters give to the School, an orrery was built.

As far as we know, four other Old Blues have served as Lord Mayor. In 1661, Sir John Frederick was the earliest Bluecoat boy to become Lord Mayor. He was MP for Dartmouth in 1660 and for the City of London in 1663. Sir John was a great benefactor to Christ's Hospital, and at his own expense rebuilt the School's hall after it was damaged in the Great Fire. In 1840, the Lord Mayor was Thomas Johnson, an Old Blue who was an oil merchant in Aldgate and a member of the Coopers' Company. Lord Mayors in 1904 and 1905 respectively, Sir John Pound and Sir Walter Vaughan Morgan, were both Old Blues. Lord Mayors have also been connected with the governance of the School; Alderman Alan Yarrow, Lord Mayor 2014–5, is a member of the Council of Almoners (that is, a Trustee) of Christ's Hospital.

Get there by bus & Tube

THE LORD MAYOR'S SHOW
SATURDAY 8 NOVEMBER 1997
0171 332 1456
www.lord-mayors-show.org.uk

For the perfect way to see the show, choose your ticket from our range of Travelcards and get unlimited travel throughout the day on the tubes, buses and trains; Family Travelcard for up to 2 adults and 4 children. Weekend Travelcard which is valid all day Saturday and Sunday or a One Day Travelcard.

Nearest Tube: Bank, Blackfriars, Mansion House, Moorgate and Temple Underground stations are all close by.
Nearest Buses: 4, 8, 11, 15, 22A, 22B, 25, 26, 35, 43, 45, 47, 48, 56, 63, 76, 133, 141, 171A, 214 and 271 all stop close to the parade.
London Travel Information 0171-222 1234

· THE PRIVILEGED REGIMENTS ·

· ANDREW WALLIS ·

IN THE SAME WAY THAT VATICAN CITY IS 'a city within a city' in Rome, so is the City of London a separate city within the capital city of England. It has its own leader in the person of the Lord Mayor, who is head of its own powerful government, the City of London Corporation, a fact little understood even by many of the people who work within its boundaries. The Crown might have had the land, but the City had the money.

Occasionally, as City workers in Moorgate head out for an early lunch they are greeted by the sound of a distant drumbeat and martial music heading towards them from City Road. Heads turning to determine the source of the noise, they stand transfixed as a military unit bearing weapons marches past. This is almost certainly one of the 'privileged regiments' exercising its right to march through the City 'with Colours flying, drums beating and bayonets fixed'. What seems to the workers in this fast-paced, high-tech financial centre to be something rather quaint and esoteric actually has its roots in a royal proclamation issued by King Edward III in 1327. To thank the Mayor and the inhabitants of the City for their frequent financial support, the King decreed the citizens of the City could no longer be dragooned into going to war. This in turn meant that press gangs or recruitment squads could no longer roam the streets of the City looking for likely candidates to force into serving the Crown. And with this decree the military chiefs of the sovereign's forces lost the right to direct regiments to march through the City without the specific permission of the Lord Mayor.

ABOVE: The Band of Her Majesty's Royal Marines in 1985.

Over the years, to acknowledge 'special relationships' forged with certain military units, the City issued warrants granting these units the 'privilege' of safe passage through the City and, as a mark of trust, allowing them to bear arms whilst so doing. Even though a regiment might possess such a privilege,

written permission is still required before entering the City boundaries and the City Marshal is still dispatched by the Lord Mayor to challenge such a body of troops as they approach.

Today most privileged regiments use the headquarters of the Honourable Artillery Company in City Road as an assembly area from which to march on the City. As the regiment approaches the City boundary at Ropemaker Street they come across the imposing, mounted figure of the City Marshal. The Commanding Officer halts the regiment and goes forward to the head of the column.

The City Marshal calls out 'Who comes there?'

The Commanding Officer then states the name of his regiment and declares they are 'exercising their ancient privilege and right to enter the City of London with Colours flying, drums beating and bayonets fixed.'

The City Marshal replies, 'I have it on the authority of the Lord Mayor to receive and attend your battalion through the City.' He salutes and leads the battalion through the City, past Mansion House to the City boundary.

The oldest regiment in the British Army is the Honourable Artillery Company, having had its already lengthy service acknowledged by the granting of a royal warrant in 1537. The regiment has had a long association with the Lord Mayor and the City of London Corporation and has come to their aid on many occasions, most famously when it deployed to defend the Lord Mayor during the Gordon Riots of June 1780. It is strange, therefore, that whilst the Honourable Artillery Company regularly exercised

its 'assumed right', no record could be found of such a grant being made, so it was not formally given the privilege until 1924.

Whilst operational commitments keep some of the privileged units from parading, there is always a strong presence in the Lord Mayor's Show of those units who enjoy this close bond with the Mayoralty and the City. All the military units who enjoy this unique bond with the City wholeheartedly enjoy the honour, almost as much as the hospitality that usually follows the reaffirmation of this wonderful privilege.

THE PRIVILEGED REGIMENTS

- The Princess of Wales's Royal Regiment
- The Royal Marines
- The Grenadier Guards
- The Royal Regiment of Fusiliers
- The Honourable Artillery Company
- The Coldstream Guards
- The Household Cavalry, comprising the Blues and Royals and the Life Guards
- The London Regiment

Having the status of a privileged regiment:
- 600 (City of London) Squadron Royal Auxiliary Air Force

These regiments are to be joined by 101 (City of London) Engineer Regiment (Explosive Ordnance Disposal) as the newest privileged regiment of the City of London sanctioned by the Court of Aldermen.

The Navy's new aircraft carrier, HMS *Queen Elizabeth*, which is due to enter service in 2020, is affiliated to the City of London.

Paul Double LVO, City Remembrancer

· WATCHING THE SHOW ·

· THE GENTLE AUTHOR ·

ONE OF THE HIGHLIGHTS OF NOVEMBER is the Lord Mayor's Show, and each year I walk over to London Wall early in the morning where this extraordinarily multifarious parade gathers, to observe the elaborate preparations at close quarters before it all moves off at eleven with the new Lord Mayor in his gleaming fairy-tale coach at its head. I cannot think of a more vibrant image of the diversity of human social endeavour – in all its paradoxes and contradictions – than this three-mile long parade which takes over an hour to pass by. The City is closed off to traffic and you walk through streets where a dreamlike hush presides

ABOVE: The Lord Mayor's State Coach at Cannon Street during the 1938 Show.

RIGHT: Watching the Show in 2007.

OPPOSITE: Watching the Show in 1884.

the river after a drunken flower girl unseated the Lord Mayor in 1711. An array of immaculately preserved historic carriages are poised with magnificent horses and freshly shaved coachmen in uniforms to match – perfect in every detail, as if they had travelled through time to be here that morning.

In 2010 I stood at the junction of Lothbury and Moorgate, at the rear of the Bank of England, to see the parade pass by. Even here the parade outnumbered those in the crowd, enforcing the sense that this was an event for the participants, not a performance for an audience but a moment of glory for those involved, in which our role was simply to be their witnesses. A costume implies an assumed identity, yet for many in the parade their clothes exemplified their roles, carrying a reality established over centuries. It took me a while to accommodate to this notion that I was not witnessing a reenactment of an historical event but the event itself. The outfits were not fancy dress – they were real.

When a marching band in ceremonial uniform comes marching straight towards you, with a hundred

to reach the assembly point where glorious chaos reigns as seven thousand overexcited participants, both military and civilian, all take the opportunity to mingle and show off their gorgeous outfits. In the time before the parade moves off, a curious photo party takes place when everyone wants their photograph taken. There is a pervasive surrealism to this situation where all are in costume and it engenders a joyful camaraderie of equals in which the boundaries of normal life dissolve.

Meanwhile down at Guildhall, in an atmosphere of high seriousness, the berobed dignitaries of the City of London are gathering, the Aldermen, the Sheriffs and the former Lord Mayors. For these people the parade is one event in an entire weekend of formal dinners and arcane rituals that attend the inauguration of the next Lord Mayor of the City of London. And in the surrounding streets, their transport awaits as it has done each year since the event was transferred from

musicians playing simultaneously, looking sharp and
displaying perfect focus, and the loud music echoes
through the narrow streets, then the vivid intricacy
of the spectacle is overwhelming. Here we were in the
heart of the ancient City of London. Soldiers returned
from recent conflict were met with cheers, and respectful
applause was forthcoming for the nurses and firemen.
From the charitable to the corporate, from the raucous
to the majestic, all the pageantry on display fused with
an inescapable emotionalism into a wondrous vision of
humanity. From the dignified seniors to the young ones
dancing on floats, and from those who take themselves
seriously to dumb clowns with painted faces, there
were so many different proposals of what it means
to be human.

· THE TELEVISION BROADCAST ·

· CATHERINE STIRK ·

IT COMES AS NO SURPRISE THAT THE historic spectacle of the Lord Mayor's Show, so rich in variety and colour, was one of the first events in the world to be broadcast live on television. The fledgling television service of the British Broadcasting Corporation (BBC) brought public occasions, such as the National Service of Remembrance at the Cenotaph and the Chelsea Flower Show, to the television audience before the onset of the Second World War.

On 2 November 1936 the BBC opened the world's first regular television service from studios and transmitters at Alexandra Palace, North London. The transmitter's range was about 35 miles. A year later the coronation procession of King George VI was broadcast to the viewing public, and then other notable events followed, such as the Lord Mayor's Show. This makes the Show one of the oldest regularly covered outside broadcast events in television history.

BELOW: The Show being filmed in 1933.

Before this time news cameramen from services such as British Pathé captured flickering black and white newsreels of the procession from as early as 1912. In these evocative newsreels you can relive different Shows from the past, including the 1921 pageant, which was blanketed with thick fog.

Over the years there have been many distinguished commentators and presenters. 2015 marks the 50th anniversary of the death of one of the BBC's finest broadcasters, Richard Dimbleby. From 1948 to 1950 he commentated on the procession as it passed through Trafalgar Square.

Throughout its broadcasting history the coverage has featured different parts of the Lord Mayor's route through the City of London. At one time the BBC's cameras were focused around St Paul's Cathedral, where the Lord Mayor pauses for a blessing before his journey continues to the Royal Courts of Justice. But 15 years ago producer Ian Russell came up with the idea of moving the cameras to Mansion House. Now the audience at home have a first-hand view of what the new Lord Mayor experiences as he or she takes the salute from those taking part.

As broadcasters we continually strive to convey the exciting atmosphere of the Show to viewers. Director Glenn Barton recently introduced the use of a Steadicam Segway, which brings a fresh and exciting perspective by allowing the camera to keep pace with the procession. The 2014 Show was not without incident – an army officer stepped into the path of the camera operator, knocking him and the camera rig off the Segway – but fortunately both emerged unscathed.

The team responsible for producing the live broadcast is small in number. It does its utmost to find out about everyone taking part, which is a daunting task for the researcher who has over a hundred floats to research, each populated with teams of dedicated people. It works hard to ensure that all the details and facts about the participants are correct, as they are at the heart of the story, in order to share them with the people watching at home. On the day itself it relies on the brilliant expertise of a large outside broadcast team, from the riggers who lay cables through the tube station in the early hours, to the floor managers, camera operators, sound supervisors and communications experts, to the exceptional runners. And of course the BBC relies on the collaboration and support of the Pageantmaster and his team, the City of London Corporation and the police. It is a great privilege for all those involved in broadcasting the Show to be part of this historic annual event, which continues to entertain with its great popularity and appeal.

ℂ · THE LORD MAYOR'S BANQUET ·

· JANE LEVI ·

FEASTING AND GOOD CHEER HAVE LONG been associated with the Lord Mayor's Show. It is said that when Henry IV processed through the City in 1399 Cheapside literally 'flowed with wine' from seven specially commissioned wine-fountains, while early illustrations show food sellers plying their wares to the crowds. The Lord Mayor's Banquet was its most famous – or, for some periods, notorious – element, known for its sumptuous menu and liberal alcohol consumption as much as for its distinguished guest list. Today, it remains a splendid but comparatively restrained affair, reaffirming the contemporary significance of this ancient role and its importance to the business community.

The banquet is now held on the Monday evening following the Show (formerly it took place in the evening of the same day). The main hall at Guildhall is laid for 700 guests, including the Aldermen, selected businesspeople, diplomats, senior judges, the late Lord Mayor, the Lord Chancellor, the Archbishop of Canterbury and the Prime Minister, the latter four of whom give speeches, as does the new Lord Mayor. Traditionally, the Prime Minister's speech on this occasion makes reference to foreign policy and is among his or her key speeches of the year, Winston Churchill's 'the end of the beginning' speech of 1942 being one of the most well-known.

ABOVE: Until the early 1900s leftovers were distributed to the poor at 12 o'clock the day after the banquet.

RIGHT: An Alderman dreams of being plagued by the animals that feature on the banquet menu. Satirising the cancellation of the Show and Lord Mayor's Banquet due to fear of riot in 1830, this lithograph is reminiscent of Henry Fuseli's *The Nightmare*.

'Traditional' menu items for the banquet have come and gone as tastes and fashions have changed. A baron of beef (the double sirloin) was a regular fixture until relatively recently, resolutely listed in English on menus otherwise written entirely in French. Small game birds such as plovers, partridges and pheasants have been classics of the English elite table since medieval times; likewise, innovative and expensive iced desserts were introduced early on and whole courses of ices given to Victorian guests. Until the mid-20th century turtle soup was always served, a tradition that can be traced back to at least the late 18th century. The lavish nature of the banquets made them a target for satire, especially in the 18th and 19th centuries, with turtles in particular appearing in comic verses and satirical prints – they were even depicted in newspaper cartoons as late as the 1930s.

RIGHT: The Lord Mayor's Banquet at Guildhall in 2014.

The style and format of the dinner itself has changed considerably over time, partly due to a Europe-wide simplification of dining styles in the 19th century. Whereas the archaic *service à la française* required large numbers of dishes to be displayed on the table for diners to choose from, *service à la russe* — the style still used today — means each diner is individually served with several fixed courses, greatly reducing the complexity of the dinners. Previously, the cooks produced literally hundreds of different dishes for each table, with the number and variety of dishes on each table being a sign of social standing: in 1727 the royal table was supplied

with 279 dishes, while the less notable tables were given a mere 26. Distinctions were also made in the ingredients used. Records for the dinner in 1634 show that the elite tables were served a first course of up to 38 dishes, including high-status swans and marchpanes (decorated marzipan cakes), while the humbler guests were given eight, including much lowlier pullets and custards.

Today's four-course dinner of a starter, fish course, main course and dessert seems extraordinarily simple in comparison, and this is a deliberate shift in emphasis. Aware that the food itself sends a message about the Corporation, ingredients for the banquet in the 21st century are excellent quality without being excessively luxurious or expensive. Gone are the days when the wastage was distributed the following day to 'the poor', though tickets for those entitled to claim these leftovers from Guildhall were still being printed into the early 1900s. However it has changed over the centuries, the banquet stands as the perfect culmination of the celebrations confirming the inauguration of the new Lord Mayor, reminding us that we still like to mark such events by sitting together over a great meal.

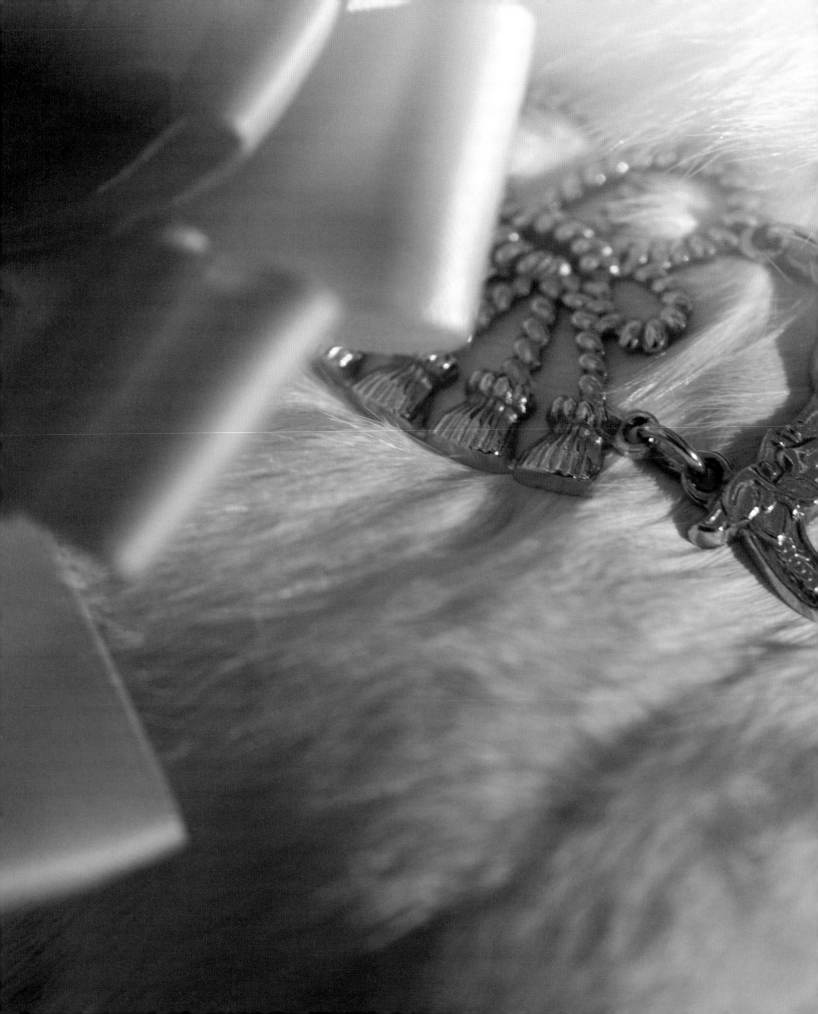

·TREASURES & PARAPHERNALIA·

PARAPHERNALIA·

Section № TWO

· THE SEAL OF THE MAYOR OF LONDON ·

· CAROLINE BARRON ·

IN THE 12TH CENTURY THE MOST important officers in London were the two Sheriffs, responsible to the people and the Crown for the good order and peace of the City. Gradually, however, the Mayor became increasingly important, and, in May 1215, a month before the barons wrung the Magna Carta from him, King John agreed to allow 'to our barons of our city of London, that they may choose to themselves every year a mayor'. Thus the Mayor came to be the most important civic officer, chosen by the citizens and, in effect, their king for a year, or for several years as was usual at first.

As the corporate government of the City developed so it became necessary for the officers chosen by the citizens to be able to act in their name. To do this it was necessary to have seals to authenticate civic documents. The corporate seal of the City of London appears to have been made at about the time of King John's charter, and its inscription records that it is the seal of the barons of London. It measured just over 7cm in diameter and was exceptionally finely engraved on both sides: it has been described as 'one of the outstanding civic seals of medieval Europe'.

As the 13th century progressed and the office of the Mayor grew in importance, it was decided that there should also be a civic seal to be used by the Mayor. This seal of the London Mayoralty first appears on a deed dated to 1277–8. It was appended to a document issued by William FitzLuke, a Durham man but also a citizen of London.

He was sealing a deed relating to land in Durham and, because his seal might not be well known in that city, he added the seal of the London Mayoralty to provide 'greater surety and testimony'. It became common for the Mayor's seal to be used in this way: to authenticate documents where the seals of parties to the agreement might not be well known.

The Mayor's seal was smaller than the City's 'great seal' and measured only 4.5cm in diameter. Moreover, it was single-sided and so cheaper and easier to use since it needed less wax. The seal shows St Paul and St Thomas Becket, the two patron saints of the City, beneath gabled arches. The saints are identified by their initials and the

PREVIOUS SPREAD: Detail of the Collar of Esses, bequeathed to the City in 1545 by Sir John Aleyn, resting on the ermine of the reception robe.

LEFT: The first seal of the Mayor of London.

ABOVE: The second seal of the Mayor of London.

three leopards of England crawl around the Gothic tabernacle in which the saints are seated. The inscription reads that it is the seal of the Mayoralty of London.

In April 1381, at a meeting of the Mayor, Aldermen and a great number of the 'more substantial commoners of the city', it was decided that the old Mayoralty Seal should be destroyed because it was 'small, crude and ancient, and ugly and unworthy of the city'. The Mayor, William Walworth, in anticipation of this decision, had already commissioned a new Mayoralty Seal. It is doubtful that the old seal was destroyed because it was 'small, crude and ancient', since it was only 100 years old and the City's Great Seal, which was older, was not destroyed. It is likely that Walworth wanted a new seal for political reasons: perhaps to signify the new order in City government which had been initiated a few years earlier, or to dissociate himself from the unpopular acts of some of the mayors who had held office earlier in the 14th century.

The new seal was larger than its predecessor and measured 6cm in diameter. It included the same visual elements as the old seal but placed them in a rather more elaborate setting. St Paul and St Thomas Becket are again seated in tabernacles in the centre of the seal but they are now flanked by two serjeants-at-arms with two angels above. In the apex of the design is an image of the Virgin Mary. An interesting innovation is the inclusion of the arms of the City supported by lions. This seems to be the first time that the City of London adopted its own armorial shield: a cross with the sword of St Paul in its first quarter. Since this seal predates the Peasants' Revolt of June 1381, the weapon in the first quarter cannot represent the dagger with which William Walworth killed Wat Tyler; yet it is easy to see how this popular myth came to be attached to the City's arms.

The arms on the seal are not, of course, coloured, but it is likely that the familiar blazon of red for the cross and the sword and silver (or white) for the ground was adopted at this time. It was also laid down during this period that the men who came to the 'Midsummer Watch' (the City's annual summer roll call) were to be dressed in red and white, and the Aldermen who accompanied the Mayor on his journey to Westminster to take his oath were also to wear scarlet and white, and so these became the City's official colours.

This 14th-century seal matrix remained in use until 1912 when it was replaced by a replica in silver to the same design but with two small Tudor roses added for distinction. The old seal matrix of 1381 was defaced by the Chamberlain in the presence of the Court of Aldermen and is now in the Museum of London. The new mayoralty seal is kept at Mansion House.

· HERALDRY IN THE LORD MAYOR'S SHOW ·

· WILLIAM HUNT ·

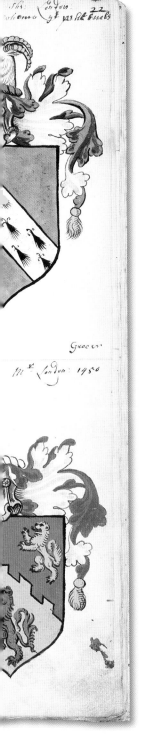

HERALDRY IN ITS PRESENT FORM BEGAN
in the 12th century, with the earliest known coat of
arms being that of Geoffrey of Anjou, dating from 1127.
As participants in tournaments became increasingly
difficult to recognize in their armour, they painted
some sort of device on their shields. These arms were
recorded by the heralds, whose job it was to organize
the tournaments, act as masters of ceremonies and
keep the score. Over the centuries the tournament
developed into an elaborate pageant, and the crest came
into being; this was made out of boiled leather or wood,
and bolted to the top of the tournament helm to add
a little extra panache to the participants' appearance.

Originally it was the landowning classes who had
arms, but then the middle classes wanted them too, as
did cities, towns and abbeys. To avoid duplicates and
squabbles the system had to be regulated, and in 1484
Richard III granted his heralds a charter of incorporation
as the College of Arms. It is perhaps significant that the
first trading corporation to petition for a grant of arms
was a London livery company, namely the Drapers'
Company, which was granted arms in 1439.

Heraldry is very much in evidence in the Lord Mayor's
Show. The arms of the participating companies are
depicted on their floats, and those of the Lord Mayor
and Sheriffs are carried on banners that accompany
their carriages. Members of 1475 (Dulwich) Squadron
of the Air Training Corps have had the privilege of
carrying these banners since 1988. Sheriffs who do
not have arms when they stand for election visit
the College of Arms to have arms designed for them.
Their shields have been hung on the wall in the Judges'
Dining Room at the Old Bailey since 1905.

The arms of the Sheriffs who have gone on to
become Lord Mayor have been recorded since 1659
in the Lord Mayor's Autograph Book, along with
his or her signature. The book came into existence
in 1846, so the earlier pages consist essentially of a
scrapbook with the entries pasted in. At the College
of Arms there is a late 17th century manuscript
depicting the arms of the Mayors, Sheriffs and
Aldermen of the City, dated in no particular order
between 1245 and 1590, with the names of their
livery companies, in most cases.

LEFT: Pages from the manuscript owned by the College of Arms
showing the arms of John Olney, Sheriff 1432–3 and Mayor 1446–7
(top left); John Gedney, Sheriff 1417–8, Mayor 1427–8 and 1447–8
(top centre-left); Thomas Chalton, Mayor 1449–50 (top centre-right);
William Whetenhall, Sheriff 1440–1 (top right); Robert Clopton,
Sheriff 1435–6 and Mayor 1441–2 (bottom left); John Hatherley
or Aderly, Sheriff 1431–2 and Mayor 1442–3 (bottom centre-left);
John Norman, Mayor 1453–4 (bottom centre-right); Nicholas
Wyfold, Mayor 1450–1 (bottom right).

· THE LORD MAYOR'S COACH ·

· BEATRICE BEHLEN ·

IN APRIL 1757 ALDERMAN SIR CHARLES Asgill ordered a 'New Grand State Coach' to be delivered on or before 29 September that year. Michaelmas was, and is, the date liverymen chose the new Lord Mayor and Asgill anticipated his election. The commission went to Joseph Berry of Leather Lane, Holborn, perhaps because his premises were near the City's borders rather than in Covent Garden where many other coachmakers worked. Budgetary constraints might also have played a role: the price was fixed at £860, contrasting with the – admittedly larger – State Coach created for King George III in 1762, which cost almost ten times as much. The Articles of Agreement stipulated the coach had to be built 'exactly to the Modell made thereof by Mr. Robert Taylor'. The architect had been enlisted the previous year for Asgill's London banking house and also designed a villa in Richmond for the merchant banker.

The Lord Mayor's coach is of the 'berlin' type, which began to replace the 'grande carosse' in the second half of the 17th century. The front and rear axles are connected by two, rather than one, beams or perches forming a chassis from which the body of the coach is suspended by four leather straps. The Agreement specified the materials to be used: 'best Ironwork' for the 'Creins', or cranes, to which the straps were attached; the panes of glass to be 'work't polished and Diamond Cutt'; and 'fine Crimson Velvet' for the lining of the coach. Berry was also asked to provide 'a very handsome Sett of Sewn Harness for Six Horses'. No wonder the coachmaker later complained that he had lost money on the commission, demanding a further £200.

In 1753 the power of the City had found expression in Mansion House for which Taylor had designed the pediment. The new carriage also served as a status symbol: the painted panels and decorative features emphasize the City's wealth and the means by which it had been amassed. The sea is represented by tritons (mythical creatures) which support the seat of the coachman who can rest his feet on a scallop shell.

BELOW: George Scharf's 1827 watercolour of the Lord Mayor's State Coach shows the tritons holding up the coachman's seat and the shell footrest.

The Lord Mayor's Coach. The Livery of the Coachman and Postilion is amongst sketches of general Costumes, quarto. This was purchased from the King

LEFT: The cherub represents
Africa. He is attached to the
coach by a scorpion and holds
a horn of plenty.

BELOW: This photograph, taken
by Henry Grant in October 1959,
shows the State Coach being
prepared for the procession.

The coach is supported at each corner by cherubs
representing Asia, Africa (*above*), America and Europe,
the then known continents.

The names of the craftsmen Berry employed are not
mentioned in the agreement but the painted panels have
long been attributed to Giovanni Battista Cipriani.
The narrative of the panels is dominated by the City's
guardian spirit, or Genius. In the top panel at the rear
she is attended by Neptune while receiving goods
from around the world. The panel below depicts what
happens next: Riches and Plenty pouring coins and
fruit into her lap. The panel on the right shows the
Genius enthroned in front of the old St Paul's receiving

a Lord Mayor presented by Fame. The left panel sees
her next to Mars, who gestures to a scroll held by
Truth bearing the name of the first Mayor of London.
The front panel depicts Hope pointing at the dome of
St Paul's Cathedral. Each main side panel is flanked
by two smaller paintings featuring the virtues Truth,
Temperance, Justice and Fortitude.

In 1805 visiting American scientist Benjamin Silliman
recorded his impressions of the Lord Mayor's Show.
He noted how the splendour of the coach was enhanced
by the plumes and ribbons of the horses and the liveries
of the coachman, footmen and postillion, who looked
'as though they had been dipped in liquid gold, and
sprinkled with fragments of diamonds'. While Silliman
remarked upon the incongruity of the then almost
50-year-old carriage, calling it an 'ancient machine, in
a style of ponderous and clumsy magnificence', he also
expressed his admiration for 'one of the most splendid
baubles that ever amused the great children of the world'.

· THE CITY'S BARGE ·

· ALEX WERNER ·

FROM THE EARLY 15TH CENTURY
the Lord Mayor and City livery companies hired
large barges, rowed by watermen, for river-borne
ceremonials and entertainments. As the conservancy
of the River Thames was entrusted to the citizens of
London through a charter of 1197, which transferred
powers from the Crown to the City to remove weirs
or obstructions in the river, it is likely that barges were
employed from around this date for official business.
The area of conservancy came to be recognized as
extending from the River Colne near Staines in the
west to Yantlet Creek in Kent in the east. The Lord
Mayor and the City of London's water-bailiff presided
over courts of conservancy in the counties of Kent,
Middlesex, Surrey and Essex and had powers to seize
unlawful fishnets and to remove encroachments that
obstructed the navigation of the river.

In 1453 the Lord Mayor, John Norman, a Draper, had
a ceremonial barge built to carry him to Westminster
to pledge his allegiance to the king. From this date,
an annual ceremonial procession took place on the
Thames with the Lord Mayor's barge accompanied
by a number of livery company and private barges.
The pageantry of the event grew especially in the
16th century. Lupold von Wedel, a German visitor to
London, recorded the spectacle of the river procession
on Lord Mayor's Day in 1584: the City's barge was
'covered in red taffettas ornamented with a white
cross', and when the Mayor stepped into it 'a salute

of more than a hundred shots was fired' and 'trumpets
and musical instruments were heard'. He explained that
'each guild or company had its own barge ornamented
with numerous flags by which each company might be
distinguished one from the other'. The City's barge was
not just employed on Lord Mayor's Day but also when
accompanying the monarch on the Thames.

The design of the Lord Mayor's barge, and the
livery company barges also, followed the structure
and build of a waterman's wherry. Clinker-built
with an extended shallow bow, the barges were
about 20m in length and evolved to include an
enclosed cabin towards the stern of the vessel where
passengers could shelter from the elements or stand
outside above on the flat roof to survey the scene.

ABOVE: *The Lord Mayor's
Show at Westminster*, 1830
by David Roberts.

BELOW: Model of
the last Lord Mayor's
barge, made by Searle
& Godfrey in 1807, on
display at the Museum
of London Docklands.

OPPOSITE: The Queen's
Row Barge *Gloriana*
passing the Palace of
Westminster in 2011.

Barge houses, especially on the south side of the river at Lambeth and Vauxhall, accommodated the vessels when they were not in use. The barges were costly to buy and maintain, requiring the employment of a bargemaster and mate. Watermen could be hired by the day with most barges requiring 18 oarsmen.

When the Conservancy Jury met in the different counties surrounding London, City officials often adjourned for dinner on board the City's barge. In July 1772, such a dinner at Twickenham was followed by music played by a band on board. The 'Duchess Dowager of Newcastle,

and some other ladies of quality' came down to the waterside to hear 'several pieces of music' played by the musicians. She ordered her butler 'to accommodate the Jury with champagne and burgundy'. Eating and drinking with toasts and music became a feature of such annual conservancy events on the City's barge. Other events where it made an appearance included ship launches and bridge openings. On 8 January 1806, when the body of Admiral Lord Nelson was carried from Greenwich to Whitehall, the vast Thames flotilla of 77 craft included the Lord Mayor's barge as well as many livery company barges.

The last City barge was built in 1807 by Searle & Godfrey of Stangate, Lambeth. With the arrival of steamboats on the Thames, the Lord Mayor's barge began to seem slightly old-fashioned. On a number of royal occasions it was even towed by a steamboat. The final river procession was held in 1856 as the management of the river passed from the City to a new body, the Thames Conservancy.

THE MODERN-DAY RIVER PAGEANT

In 2010 the Lord Mayor returned to the River Thames and travelled to the City in the morning, prior to the main event. This has continued each year since: he or she is transported aboard the Queen's Row Barge *Gloriana*, accompanied by a flotilla of traditional barges and small boats, echoing the spectacular river celebrations that ended in the mid-1800s.

Malcolm Knight

⟪ · GOG AND MAGOG ·

· DOMINIC REID ·

LEFT: The wooden Magog carved by Captain Richard Saunders in 1708; destroyed in the Blitz.

GOG AND MAGOG, TWO ENORMOUS BUT benevolent giants, are the traditional guardians of the City of London and have been carried in the Lord Mayor's Show since the reign of Henry V. They are descended from the pagan giants of early English pageantry and their history is buried in myth and legend.

The story goes that Diocletian had 33 wicked daughters, for whom he found 33 husbands to curb their wilful ways. His daughters were not happy. They plotted under the leadership of the eldest, and slit the throats of their husbands as they slept. For this appalling crime they were set adrift in a boat with half a year's rations, and after a long and dreadful journey they arrived at some islands which came to be called Albion after Alba, the eldest sister. Here they lived and cohabited with demons, and produced a race of evil giants. And so we come to hear of a group of wild windswept islands inhabited by giants.

Many early peoples regarded the original inhabitants of their territory as giants, and the memory of these early races was preserved in mythology. Heroes became giants in the popular mind. They were often large and powerful men, and their physical strength and stature became exaggerated as their deeds passed into saga. These pagan giants were not ugly or deformed; they were simply giant men.

The story continues that Brutus, the great-grandson of Aeneas, fled from Troy and after a series of adventures arrived in these islands, which he renamed Britain, after himself. With him he brought his most able warrior and champion Corineus, who fought the leader of the 'Giant brood' in single combat, and slew him by hurling him from a high rock into the sea. The name of the giant was Gogmagog and the rock from which he was thrown became known as Langoëmagog or 'The Giants Leap'. As a reward Corineus was given the western part of the island, which was named after him: Cornwall. But Brutus travelled east, where he built a city he called Troya Nova, or New Troy, and which came to be known as London.

At one time human sacrifice was common, but as times grew more civilized, images of men were burned instead of the men themselves. The custom of carrying such effigies at festivals became widespread, not only in England but on the continent. These giants of pageantry are the last vestiges of the pagan effigies. Gog and

ABOVE: Gog and Magog made of polystyrene and transported on Mini Mokes in the 1973 Show.

Magog have no trace of the supernatural about them – they originated in folk custom, deriving their names from mythological characters. They are a part of a tradition in English pageantry that predates Christianity.

An alternative version of the story has it that these giants were the last two survivors of the sons of the 33 daughters of Diocletian, who were captured and chained to the gates of a palace on the site of Guildhall to act as its guardians. However they got there, we know that by the reign of Henry V, there were giants residing in Guildhall. And when in 1554 they appeared in the Lord Mayor's Show, the names Gogmagog and Corineus were attached to them for the first time.

RIGHT: Gog, made of wicker by the Worshipful Company of Basketmakers in 2006.

In 1605 the Pageantmaster of the day alluded to the giants who appeared in the procession as Corineus and Gogmagog. And later in 1672, the Pageantmaster Thomas Jordan referred to them as 'two exceeding rarities', and stated that 'at the conclusion of the Show, they are to be set up in Guildhall, where they may be daily seen all year and I hope never to be demolished by such dismal violence as happened to their predecessors.' He was referring to the destruction of the City by the Great Fire. But his giants lasted only a few years, being made of wickerwork and pasteboard, like their sacrificial forebears, and were destroyed by mice and rats. They were replaced in 1708 by a magnificent pair of wooden statues carved by Captain Richard Saunders that survived for over 200 years before their destruction in the Blitz. These, in turn, were replaced by the pair which can now be seen in Guildhall, and which were carved by David Evans in 1953 as a gift to the City of London by Alderman Sir George Wilkinson. Wilkinson had been Lord Mayor in 1940, the year of the destruction of their predecessors.

This is the most recent of their rebirths, symbolized by the phoenix on Magog's shield, representing return after fire. Today the words of Thomas Boreman in his *Gigantick History* of 1741 still ring true:

> Corineus and Gogmagog were two brave giants who richly valued their honour and exerted their whole strength and force in the defence of their liberty and country; so the City of London, by placing these, their representatives in their Guildhall, emblematically declare, that they will, like mighty giants, defend the honour of their country and liberties of this their City; which excels all others, as much as those huge giants exceed in stature the common bulk of mankind.

· THE SWORDS AND MACES OF THE CITY OF LONDON ·

· JAMES NORTH ·

WHILST THERE ARE A NUMBER OF CITIES
in the United Kingdom which have the privilege of
having a sword borne before their Mayor, the City
of London is unique in not only being the oldest to
enjoy this tradition but also in having a number of
ceremonial swords to be used on different occasions,
each with its own history. The Sword of State has
been supplemented by a Sword of Justice at the
Central Criminal Court, by a Pearl Sword for the
most important of ceremonial occasions and by a
Mourning Sword for periods of solemnity.

The office of Swordbearer was first officially recorded
in 1417, but probably has much older roots. The
current incumbent is only the 57th since that date to
hold the office. On ceremonial occasions in the City,
the Swordbearer carries the Sword of State directly in
front of the Lord Mayor. The sword is 51 inches long,
covered in deep red velvet and decorated with silver gilt
badges showing the arms of the City and other heraldic
devices. The original Sword of State was made in 1680,
with a silver gilt pommel wrought with the figures
of Justice and Fame. In 1962 a replica with identical
decorations was commissioned, and this is now used
on a regular basis due to the antiquity of the original.

The Sword of State is usually carried alongside the
Great Mace, made in 1735 by John White of London
on the order of the Court of Aldermen. It is carried by
the Common Cryer and Serjeant-at-Arms, an office

ABOVE: Sir Maurice Jenks, Lord Mayor, and Sir William Phené
Neal, Late Lord Mayor, holding the Mace in Guildhall on Lord
Mayor's Day 1931.

RIGHT: The 1680 Sword of State.

which goes back to at least 1291. Previous versions of
the current mace stretch back to 1559; it is unclear what
the Serjeant carried before that time. The current mace
is silver gilt, surmounted by a royal crown bearing the
orb and cross. Further decorative work below
the crown includes a rose, thistle, fleur-de-
lis and a harp, and the cipher of George
III. The mace represents the authority of
the sovereign; in the physical presence of the
monarch it is covered or carried reversed.

Tradition states that the Pearl Sword was given by
Elizabeth I to the City at the opening of the first Royal
Exchange in 1571. It has a crimson scabbard covered

in more than 2,000 pearls, with a golden hilt and an intricate pommel. On great ceremonial occasions, usually at St Paul's Cathedral, the Pearl Sword is carried by the Lord Mayor who processes in front of the sovereign, having been previously surrendered to the monarch as a symbol of the City's continuing loyalty to the Crown.

The Mourning Sword is without ornament and it used for occasions of mourning and special solemnity. It was used at the funeral of Baroness Thatcher in 2013 and before that at the funeral of Sir Winston Churchill in 1965, both at St Paul's Cathedral, when the Lord Mayor of the day carried the sword in front of Her Majesty the Queen. According to legend, the blade is 16th century and was found in the mud of the Thames. It is fixed onto a 19th-century hilt and guard of black japanned iron. As early as 1534 there is a reference to the purchase of a sword with a black velvet sheath to replace earlier mourning swords, which were used more frequently then than now, including on Good Friday.

❡ · THE COLLAR OF ESSES ·

· MARIA HAYWARD ·

SERVING AS A SYMBOL OF CIVIC AUTHORITY AND OF
loyalty to the Crown, the Collar of Esses worn by the Lord Mayor of London
is a beautiful piece of 16th-century goldsmith's work. Bequeathed to the City of
London in 1545 by the Mercer Sir John Aleyn, the collar has ten enamelled
Tudor roses alternating with nine double knots or friar's knots
and twenty S's. However the c.1574 illustration by Lucas de
Heere depicts 14 knots and roses, indicating that the collar
has undergone a series of alterations. One of the most
significant was the addition in 1607 of the oval pendant
depicting the City's arms in cameo. The arms are
surrounded by a blue enamelled garter with
the City's motto *Domine dirige nos*
and set with diamonds. The central
portcullis may also date to 1607
or slightly later.

Sanctus' (Holy Spirit), or 'Seneschallus' (high steward) and/or 'Seigneur'. Even so, the association with the Lancastrians is clearer. When John of Gaunt and his retainers were attacked in 1377 the London mob took the Collars of Esses worn by the duke's retinue. Consequently, the earl of Arundel linked Richard II's adoption of the Collar of Esses in 1394 to the excessive influence of his uncle. In 1416 Sigismund, Holy Roman emperor, wore the Collar of Esses to demonstrate his allegiance to Henry V when he came to England to be made a Knight of the Garter and to make a treaty against the French. In contrast, the Yorkists adopted collars of roses and suns, with a pendant of a white lion for Edward IV and a white boar for Richard III.

A range of collars were worn at the Tudor court. Sir Thomas More, Henry VIII's Lord Chancellor, was painted in 1527 wearing a collar of single S's with a pair of portcullises and pendant red rose. In the same year Sir Henry Guildford was painted in the collar of the Order of the Garter, while the king also had the collars of the Burgundian Order of the Golden Fleece and the French Order of St Michael. In addition Henry VIII favoured heavily jewelled collars which were exclusive to the monarch.

Mayoral collars continue to act as a potent visual symbol of the wearer's authority. As such the Collar of Esses has been worn by successive Lord Mayors of London as they have undertaken their duties since Aleyn's bequest. To keep the collar in place when worn over the official robes it is tied on with ribbons. This regular use has resulted in the delicate 16th-century collar being repaired a number of times. In 1981 a gold replica chain was presented by five former mayors, so ensuring that Aleyn's collar will continue to act as a jewel in the Lord Mayor's collection.

ABOVE: The 1802 Badge worn by the Lord Mayor, either attached to the Collar of Esses or on a neck ribbon.

OPPOSITE: Detail of the Collar of Esses resting on the scarlet gown.

Refer to pages 75 and 76 to see the Collar worn with the robes and tied in place.

Although Aleyn served as Lord Mayor in 1525 and 1535, the collar was already an integral part of the mayoral regalia. When Charles V, king of Spain and Holy Roman emperor, made his formal entry into London on 29 May 1533, it was recorded that 'the Maior and his bretherne [were] all in Scalet and furs, [those] as were knightes had collers of Esses and the Remnant having good chaeynes'. Who made the collar for Aleyn is uncertain but most items of this kind were the work of the royal goldsmiths such as Morgan Wolf. In March 1541 Wolf was paid £73 17s 8½d for 'a collar of gold with esses'. They varied in weight and design. The collar given to Sir Edward Montagu by Henry VIII in c.1546 did not have roses.

The meaning of the letter 'S' is much debated. Suggestions include 'sanctus' (holy) or 'Spiritus

· THE CAP OF MAINTENANCE ·

· MARIA HAYWARD ·

A CAP OF MAINTENANCE, OFTEN IN conjunction with the honour of having a sword which could be borne before its Mayor, was granted to London and 16 other towns and cities in England and Ireland from the 14th century onwards by the monarch as a symbol of the bond between the civic authorities and the Crown. The significance of this relationship was made clear when Henry VII granted a cap and sword to Exeter in 1497 'to encourage the mayor and citisens to be myndefull of their duties and to continue dutyfull and obedient subgects ... with a hatte of maintenaunce to be borne before him and his successors as it is used in the Citie of London'.

As the surviving caps of maintenance from Exeter (1497), Waterford (1536) and York (granted by Richard II in 1388, replaced in 1445 and again in 1580) indicate, they are more of a hat than a cap in terms of shape. They have a fairly tall crown with straight sides, a flat top and a fairly wide circular brim. Made from crimson silk velvet and decorated with metal thread embroidery, they are well suited to their ceremonial function. A similar cap was carried in front of the king when he processed to the opening of parliament. The parliament roll of 1512 produced by the Garter king of arms depicts the Duke of Buckingham carrying the cap of maintenance in front of Henry VIII dressed in his parliament robes consisting of a scarlet robe, kirtle, hood and cap.

In 1546 the Mayor of London gave a 'goodly and ryche' hat to the Swordbearer, and this may well be the 'rich

ABOVE:
Sir Thomas Vezey Strong,
Lord Mayor 1910–11,
accompanied, from left to
right, by his Swordbearer
(wearing the cap of
maintenance), the
City Marshal, and
the Common Cryer
and Serjeant-at-Arms
holding the Mace.

hat of crimson velvet called the cap of maintenance' that was repaired in 1614. In addition, from 1520 the Swordbearer was provided with a cap of grey fur for the winter and of white silk for the summer as well as a gown. The Swordbearer was depicted in a tall grey fur hat by Lucas de Heere in 1574 and in a smaller fur cap in illustrations from 1598 and 1620 which may reflect the two different hats he was given.

Gradually the fur hat worn by the Swordbearer, sometimes described as a Muscovy hat, became known as the cap of maintenance. The significance of the fur hat was indicated by it being incorporated into the arms of the City from the late 17th century

as an alternative crest to the gold wreath and silver dragon's wing (the left or sinister wing). It is a tall sable hat with no brim. Viewed from the front the sides slope outwards from the band to the flat crown. The current hat, or cap, was made in 1975 and there is a small pocket in the lining to keep the key to the seal of Christ's Hospital, established in 1552 during the Mayoralty of Sir Richard Dobbs. At the end of the Silent Ceremony, held on the day before the Lord Mayor's Show, the Lord Mayor leaving office takes the key from the Swordbearer and gives it to the new Lord Mayor, who returns it to the Swordbearer, who in turn agrees to 'keep it under his hat'.

Finally it is worth noting the small cap of maintenance sewn to the back of the Mayor's scarlet gown. It is stitched to the right side of the back yoke and it is a vestigial cap, alluding to the significance of the mayoral office. Shaped rather like a nightcap, it is made from black silk velvet, with a crimson silk lining and a wide decorative band of the same around the lower edge. There is a small, round decorative motif, half-black, half-crimson.

RIGHT: The Swordbearer as depicted by Lucas de Heere in c.1574.

·THE LORD MAYOR'S ROBES·

·MARIA HAYWARD·

Mayer, of alderman die
Mayer gheweest is.

Alderman

Een va de
Lineraye
ziet vooet
folio 8. page 2

THE MAYOR OF LONDON, ALONG WITH the Mayors of Bristol and York, was mentioned in the sumptuary legislation for 1402 as having scarlet robes of office. The function of these robes was to mark out the Mayor from other citizens. As such the robes were well suited to assert the importance of the City, and to differentiate the Mayor in civic ceremonies such as the Midsummer Watch. According to *The Singularities of London* by L. Genade, the Lord Mayor was elected from the Aldermen who were 'distinguished from the rest of the people by their long robes of scarlet red or violet worn on feast days and on working days by a black mob-cap 4 large fingers wide'. Lucas de Heere illustrated the full-length scarlet robes in the 1570s. Faced with sable, with half-length sleeves edged with fur, in tandem with full length hanging sleeves, the cut was modelled on that of the fashionable male gown. In some cities, including Winchester, Mayor's wives also had a scarlet gown.

The status of the Lord Mayor of London has been expressed more recently by his having several sets of robes for specific occasions. First there are the scarlet and violet gowns, both of which have links to Aldermanic robes. The scarlet gown is

LEFT: Lucas de Heere's c.1574 illustration of the Lord Mayor of London with an Alderman and a Liveryman.

OPPOSITE: The scarlet gown.

RIGHT: The black and gold robe and detail.

BELOW: The violet gown.

BELOW RIGHT: The reception robe.

made from fulled scarlet wool trimmed with dark brown fur down both fronts and around the opening of the main sleeve, forming a deep cape collar and edged with a single guard of black silk velvet around the hem and on the sleeves. These are two part sleeves, with the main sleeve and the full length hanging sleeves. The gown has a train and it is lined with cream silk satin. The current violet gown is made from wool that is almost black and it is worn for Common Council meetings and at the Silent Ceremony, which takes place on the Friday before the Lord Mayor's Show. It is trimmed with a black velvet guard and faced with a rather coarse dark fur.

BELOW: Sir Rupert de la Bère, Lord Mayor 1952–3, in the coronation robe.

Much more sumptuous is the ankle length reception robe which is made from crimson velvet, has an ermine cape, is ornamented with gold cords and tassels and has two white satin rosettes on each shoulder to hold the Collar of Esses. It is lined with white satin. This robe is principally worn at state banquets hosted by the Lord Mayor and the City of London at Guildhall in honour of a head of state during his or her official visit to the United Kingdom as the guest of the monarch. It is also worn for the Pearl Sword (and more infrequently the Mourning Sword) ceremony in the presence of the monarch at St Paul's Cathedral.

The black and gold robe is worn on various state or City occasions including major church services, commemoration or speech days at City schools and at the Lord Mayor's Banquet. The robe has hanging sleeves with a slit opening for the arm to pass through decorated with gold thread embroidery and very ornate gold passementerie. The black silk damask robe trimmed with gold braid owned by Sir Walter Henry Wilkin, Lord Mayor 1895–6, is now in the Museum of London. The office of the Lord Mayor's trainbearer was abolished in 1860, so while the robes all have trains they are usually looped up and fastened with a button and loop inside the left sleeve of the gown.

Two other items deserve mention. First the Lord Mayor's coronation robe which, like the reception robe, is of rich crimson velvet; it is lined throughout with white corded silk and has four horizontal bands of gold braid and ermine on each front. It is edged with gold lace and has two white satin rosettes. While peers' robes have a cape of ermine, the Lord Mayor's robe is decorated with four wide horizontal bands of gold braid and spotted ermine. As such they are distinctive while serving to stress the importance of the Lord Mayor. Second is the Lord Mayor's black plush tricorn hat trimmed with black ostrich feathers and burnished steel ornaments.

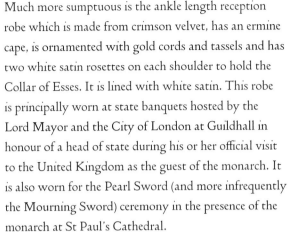

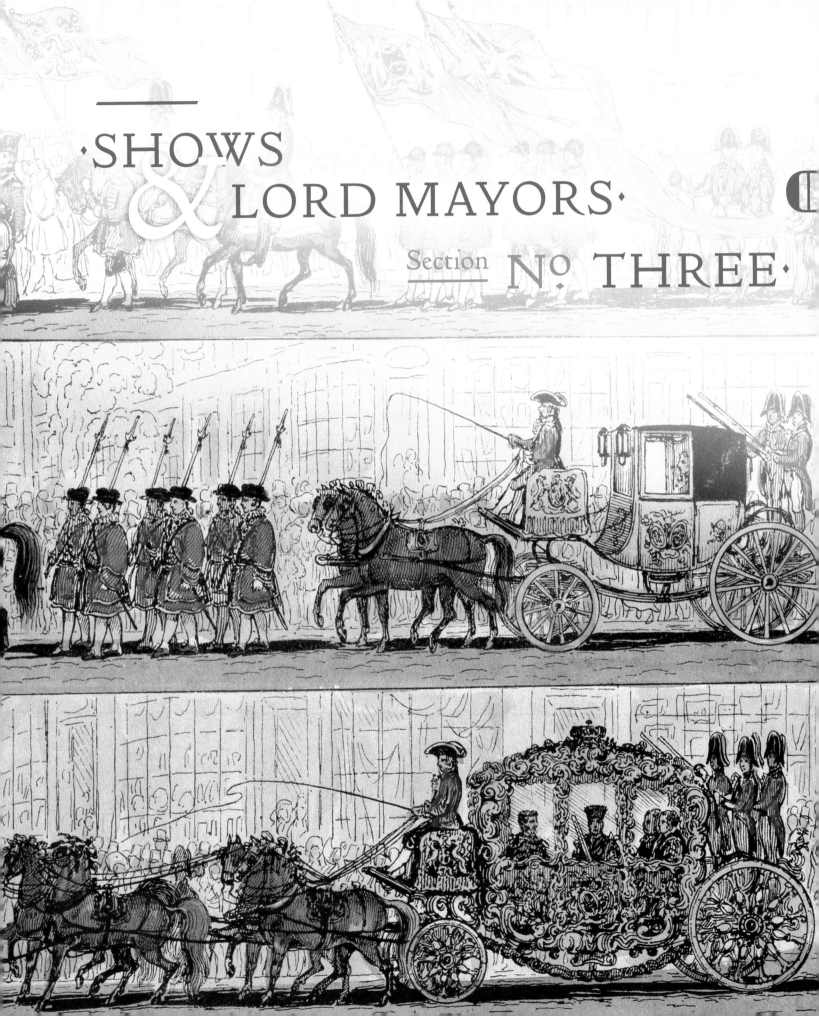

· WILLIAM WALWORTH AND THE PEASANTS' REVOLT ·

· CAROLINE BARRON ·

WILLIAM WALWORTH WAS, LIKE SO MANY Londoners in the medieval period, an immigrant. He came originally from County Durham and was apprenticed to a wealthy Fishmonger, John Lovekyn. The Fishmongers not only dealt wholesale with fish, the staple medieval diet, but they also owned ships and engaged in overseas trade. Lovekyn was a very successful merchant who was elected as Mayor of the City on three occasions. Before he died in 1368 he appointed his ex-apprentice as one of his executors, and Walworth, now a rising merchant himself, also succeeded his old master as the Alderman of Bridge ward. Walworth's rise was rapid: in 1370 he was elected as one of the City's Sheriffs, and four years later he was elected Mayor for the first time. He also served four times as one of the City's MPs.

So when Walworth was elected Mayor of London for the second time in October 1380 he had already had extensive experience of city government. But this was a period of considerable unrest in London and the 'radicals' had recently secured far-reaching changes in the way the City was governed. These included the annual election of Aldermen, who thus changed every year rather than serving for life as had been customary. This may well have spread authority more widely but it introduced an element of instability and inexperience into the higher level of city government. So it was a restless and poorly-governed city that faced the rebels in June 1381.

There is no surviving formal record of what the rebels wanted: only the accounts to be found in the – largely hostile – monastic chronicles. But some of their objectives were expressed in the demands made to the king at Mile End and Smithfield. The Black Death of 1348–9 had radically changed the balance of economic power in England. It seems that at least a third, and possibly a half, of the population of England had died during the outbreak of plague. In consequence there was an acute shortage of labour: in spite of government legislation, wages began to rise and peasants who were free (as opposed to serfs who were tied to their estates) were able to move to seek better working conditions elsewhere. Many of the peasants who rose in 1381 were those who had been unable, because they were serfs, to benefit from the changed economic climate: they banded together in an attempt to shake off their servile status, take advantage of the new economic opportunities and seek a fairer distribution of wealth.

On Thursday 13 June 1381, the feast of Corpus Christi, Richard II sailed downstream to Blackheath to negotiate with the men from Kent. When they would not disperse Richard returned to the safety of the Tower of London, and the rebels swarmed into Southwark and then across London Bridge, where the drawbridge was let down by Alderman Walter Sybyle, not out of sympathy for the rebels but in panic lest they should fire the Bridge. In the same way the Alderman guarding Aldgate allowed the Essex rebels to enter the City. Walworth was probably not on the scene to strengthen their resolve because he was with the king in the Tower. Certainly he accompanied the king when he rode out the next day to meet the rebels at Mile End. But although some of the rebels went home believing they had secured their objectives by the new charters of freedom that Richard had granted, many others, led by the Kentishman, Wat Tyler, remained. Archbishop Sudbury, the Chancellor, and Robert Hales, prior of the Hospitallers and Treasurer, were dragged from the Tower and beheaded. Many immigrant Flemings were murdered that day and there was general mayhem in the City. But an attempt to burn Guildhall had failed and the City's rulers were beginning to organize resistance to the violence.

Friday 15 June marked the climax of the revolt in London. Richard first visited Westminster Abbey and then, thus fortified, rode with a party to Smithfield, located northwest of the City. Here Wat Tyler and the men of Kent were lined up on the west side of the field and the king and his party, which included William Walworth and his Swordbearer, John Blyton, occupied the east side near to the Priory buildings. Richard ordered Walworth to summon Wat Tyler to come to speak with him. When he rode up Tyler shook the king by the hand in a familiar way and called him 'brother'. When asked why he and his men would not go home, Tyler produced a list of

radical demands which included the abolition of serfdom and the disendowment of the Church. Richard agreed to these, saving his 'regality'. At this point a scuffle broke out, possibly predetermined by the royal party. Tyler may have provoked a reaction by behaving in a provocative way, calling for a drink and then washing out his mouth and spitting on the ground. Someone in the royal entourage called Tyler a thief and a robber and when Tyler tried to strike his accuser, Walworth intervened, 'reasoned with him for his violent behaviour and contempt done in the king's presence', and attempted to arrest him. Blyton ordered Tyler to take down his hood while in the king's presence and thus, trapped and provoked, Tyler stabbed at Walworth, who was wearing armour under his gown and so was unhurt. In retaliation he wounded Tyler seriously in the neck, and Tyler was then dealt a mortal blow by a member of the king's entourage. He rode a little way forward on his horse and fell to the ground. The rebels saw their leader mortally wounded

ABOVE: A manuscript illumination from Jean Froissart's *Chroniques* from the last quarter of the 15th century depicting the death of Wat Tyler. William Walworth wields the sword; Richard II and his esquire look on.

ABOVE RIGHT: Copy letters patent of Richard II withdrawing all grants made to the rebels during the Peasants' Revolt, and commanding the Sheriff and other officers to proclaim the same.

and were about to shoot their arrows at the royal party when Richard rode forward, and, with considerable courage and presence of mind, called to the rebels that he was now their leader and that they should follow him. He turned his horse north towards Clerkenwell Fields and the men of Kent followed him.

Walworth rode back into the City and summoned the Aldermen to bring the well-armed men of their wards out to Clerkenwell to support the king and disperse the rebels. Walworth himself returned to St Bartholomew's where Tyler had been taken, dying, into the Master's lodgings in the hospital. Walworth dragged the rebel leader out into Smithfield and executed him, and then rode on to Clerkenwell to display the head to the rebels. Now that their leader was dead and they were faced with a strong force of armed Londoners, the rebels begged for mercy. Richard refused to allow the armed men to fall on the rebels and instead ordered that they should be escorted back through London and across the Bridge, and so home to Kent.

The crisis was over, although much mopping-up remained to be done. Meanwhile Richard acknowledged his debt to the Londoners who had finally rallied to his support. There and then he knighted William Walworth and four other Aldermen. Walworth protested that he should not be knighted because 'he was only a merchant and had to live by his trade', but his protest was ignored. In fact Walworth had extensive property in London, which he bequeathed to his wife Margaret when he died in 1386. He also established a chantry in his parish church of St Michael Crooked Lane, where the priest was to pray for Walworth, his wife and for Walworth's late master, John Lovekyn. Unusually among London merchants, Walworth had a considerable library containing religious books and volumes on law. His house in Thames Street, where Lovekyn had once lived, went to Walworth's own apprentice, and then became the site of Fishmongers' Hall. As well as being the Mayor of London in 1381 and the executioner of Wat Tyler, Walworth's will suggests that he was an exceptionally pious and learned London merchant.

· RICHARD 'DICK' WHITTINGTON ·

· CAROLINE BARRON ·

RICHARD WHITTINGTON WAS PROBABLY the most famous of all the medieval London Mayors. His renown rests in part on what he achieved in his lifetime (c.1356–1423) and in part on his adoption in the late 16th century as the hero of a story in which a cat brings fame and fortune to a penniless London apprentice. There were reasons why Whittington was chosen to star in this later tale and pantomime.

Richard Whittington was the son (but not the eldest son) of Sir William Whittington, a knight from Pauntley in Gloucestershire. Since he was unlikely to inherit the family manors, Richard made his way to London to seek his fortune and became apprenticed to a mercer (merchants who traded in luxury materials imported from Italy). Many Londoners in this period were immigrants from the countryside, but Richard was unusual in coming from the gentry class. Later in life he bore the arms of the Whittingtons of Pauntley but with an annulet or ring on the shield to show that he was a fourth son.

It may be that his gentry origins helped him to find noble customers in the capital, but his breakthrough appears to have come in 1392 when he sold mercery worth over £3,000 to the wardrobe of King Richard II. Richard Whittington clearly knew what his customers wanted and was able to

fulfil their desire for cloths of gold and rich velvets. His growing wealth led him into the export trade in wool (England's major export at the time) and also into lending money to the Crown. In the era before banking, the royal government often had cash flow problems and needed the wealthy city merchants to provide loans in advance of the slow returns from parliamentary taxation. These royal loans were not repaid with interest (which was contrary to the rulings of the Church), but the lenders might be rewarded with offices and other privileges and perquisites.

There is no doubt that Richard Whittington became very wealthy; he also appears to have got on well with Richard II. When the King thought the City was badly governed in June 1397 he insisted on choosing a new Mayor (who was normally elected by the citizens) and selected Whittington. The following October the Londoners prudently elected Richard as Mayor, and did so again in 1406 and 1419. Thus Whittington was indeed 'thrice Lord Mayor of London', and this was extremely rare by this time. In the 15th century only eleven Londoners served twice as Mayor and none served three times.

Richard Whittington married Alice, the daughter of a Dorset knight, Sir Ivo Fitzwarren – again indicating his gentry rather than mercantile connections. Alice died in 1410 and, unusually, Richard did not marry again.

LEFT: A scene from the pantomime legend of Dick Whittington, c.1870.

LEFT: An 18th-century chapbook illustration of Dick Whittington, his household and his cat.

of Priests in his parish church of St Michael Paternoster Royal and also an almshouse for 13 poor men and women nearby. It was customary for such charitable institutions to be administered by the Church but Richard instead chose the Company of Mercers to run his college and almshouse, thus setting a precedent for the charitable enterprises of the City livery companies. Whittington's name was attached to his college and almshouse and in this way his fame lived on in the City. When the European fable of a cat bringing good fortune to a poor man reached England in the late 16th century, in London it was associated with the famous and charitable Richard Whittington who had died 150 years earlier.

Truth and fable are mixed together in the pantomime of Dick Whittington: he was an immigrant to London; he married Alice Fitzwarren, but she was not the daughter of a London merchant; he was Mayor of London three times; and he did lend money to the King and was conspicuously charitable. But he was not a poor boy and he did not (so far as we know) have a cat with which he ventured on a ship to Barbary. Yet he was considered by his fellow Londoners to be outstanding, and, in the words of a contemporary poem, he was of all merchants the 'lode star [guiding light] and chief chosen flower'.

ABOVE: An early 17th-century engraving of Richard Whittington by Renold Elstrack.

He and Alice had no surviving children and so he made extensive and innovative plans for the disposal of his fortune (over £5,000 in cash and plate) after his death. Among other charitable enterprises he endowed a College

C · COMMENTATORS AND EYEWITNESS ACCOUNTS ·

· TRACEY HILL ·

THE EARLY MODERN SHOW WAS A renowned spectacle that drew a vast audience from home and abroad. As well as lining the streets in large numbers, spectators also crowded the banks of the Thames to watch the lavishly decorated barges and galley foist [a small galley loaded with guns], and the river itself would have been full of smaller vessels bearing sightseers. Visitors to London often included the Show in their itineraries, and as a result there are a number of eyewitness accounts of the pageantry. These spectators give fascinating impressions of the vivid colour and raucous noise of the entertainments.

One of the earliest commentators was the Merchant Taylor, Henry Machyn, in the mid-16th century. Machyn's 'chronicle' preserves descriptions of a period of civic pageantry about which relatively little else is known. In 1553, for example, he recounted a dizzying combination of music, cannons, coloured banners, traditional characters such as the devil, and fireworks:

> then cam xvj trumpeters blohyng ... and then cam
> a duyllyll [devil], and after cam the bachelars all
> in a leveray [livery], and skar lett hods; and then
> cam the pagant of sant John Baptyst gorgyusly, with
> goodly speches; and then cam all the kynges trumpeters
> blowhyng, and evere trumpeter havyng skarlet capes.

Machyn was a Londoner and therefore familiar with civic figures such as the Companies' liverymen. Other overseas eyewitnesses struggled to make sense of what they saw. The German traveller Lupold von Wedel, for instance, confessed that he only remembered part of the 1585 Show, writing that 'one of [the characters was] holding a book, another a pair of scales, the third a sceptre. What the others had I forget'.

In another instance, a foreign spectator was more interested in the behaviour of the crowd. Orazio Busino, chaplain to the Venetian ambassador, wrote a long and detailed report on the 1617 Show, emphasizing the 'surging mass of people' and the mixture of apprentices, 'painted wenches' and 'old men in their dotage' who thronged the streets. One pageant, he recorded, featured a man playing a Spaniard, who decided to improvise

BELOW: Abram Booth's sketch of 'Apollo's palace', 1629.

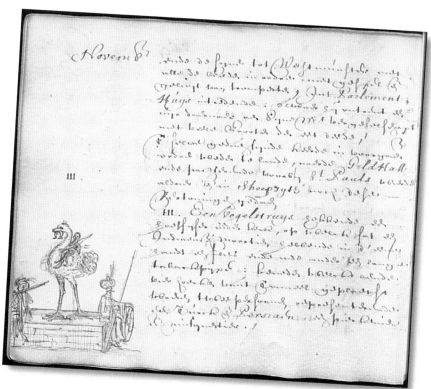

by, apparently, 'kissing his hands, right and left, but especially to the Spanish ambassador ... in such wise as to elicit roars of laughter from the multitude'. Anti-Spanish sentiment was indeed then prevalent in London, with controversial negotiations over a marriage between Prince Charles and the Spanish Infanta underway. Busino went on to describe an altercation when an outraged woman struck a Spaniard thought to be part of the ambassador's party 'with a bunch of greens', leaving the unfortunate man's fine garments 'embroidered' with 'soft, fetid mud'.

There are not just written recollections of the Shows: a Dutch visitor to the City in 1629, Abram Booth, made sketches of the pageant devices in his 'Journael' which bear out the printed descriptions in Dekker's book *Londons Tempe*. Booth's drawings from life, such as the Indian boy on an ostrich and 'Apollo's palace', bring the spectacle back to life and demonstrate that the large sums disbursed on these occasions were well spent.

In the 1660s, however, the appeal had diminished for some. The diarist Samuel Pepys witnessed the first Show after the Restoration but was not overwhelmed, recording in his diary that 'the pageants ... were many, and I believe good, for such kind of things, but in themselves but poor and absurd'. In 1661 and 1662 he missed the Show due to other commitments; the following year he attended the Guildhall dinner and then 'took coach and through Cheapside, and there saw the pageants, which were very silly'. In 1665 and 1666, of course, there was no full-scale Show, which is a subject to be explored elsewhere.

THE SHOW IN THE ELIZABETHAN ERA ·

· TRACEY HILL ·

THE LORD MAYOR'S SHOW CAME TO TRUE prominence in the 1610s and 1620s, but the groundwork for those splendid entertainments was laid in the late Elizabethan period. Only three printed pageant books survive from pre-1600: George Peele's *The Device of the Pageant* (1585) and *Descensus Astraeae* (1591), and Thomas Nelson's *The deuice of the pageant* (1590). These books, although lacking in the elaborate detail one finds in the Jacobean and Caroline works, are our main source of evidence for the nature of the pageantry in those early days.

George Peele, known nowadays chiefly as the author of the play *The Battle of Alcazar*, followed the lead of

his father James, who had produced speeches for Christopher Draper's mayoral inauguration in 1566. Richard Mulcaster, the first headmaster of the Merchant Taylors' School, wrote the speeches for 1568 and, quite probably, 1561 too; he is likely also to have composed speeches in English and Latin for Elizabeth I's coronation entry into the City a decade previously, as well as acting in the same capacity for King James' entry in 1604.

The Elizabethan Show followed the broad format of later Shows, with pageant devices accompanied by speeches declaiming the civic virtues expected of the new incumbent. In 1590 costumed actors delivered speeches either in the persona of some aspect of good

ABOVE: The statue of William Walworth at Holborn Viaduct in the City of London.

civic governance such as 'Wisedome', 'Plentie' and 'Loialtie and Concord', or whilst sat on heraldic beasts like the unicorn. As 1590 was a Fishmongers' Company year, naturally the Company's greatest hero William Walworth took centre stage. Accompanied by some of the other main protagonists of the 1381 Peasants' Revolt, King Richard II and Jack Straw, Walworth reminded the watching crowds of his momentous deed: 'I slew Jacke Straw, who sought my kings disgrace / and for

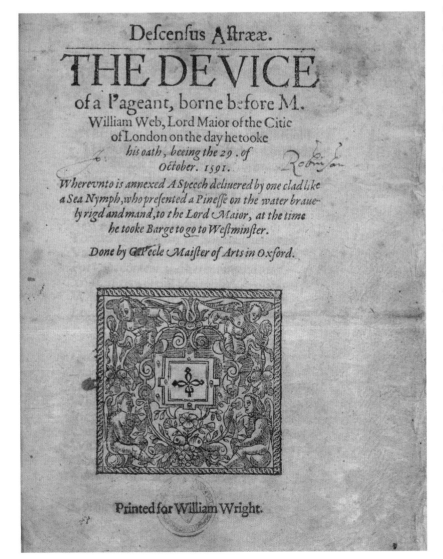

my act reapt honors of great prize'. The speech actually makes two significant errors: Walworth killed Wat Tyler, not Jack Straw, and the dagger in the City's arms refers to St Paul rather than the Fishmonger Lord Mayor, but it is unlikely that many would have noticed on the day.

George Peele's Show for Wolstan Dixie in 1585 was also composed of a sequence of speeches focused around one pageant only, without the more complex narrative structures one finds in the later Shows. A character dressed as a Moor and sat on a 'luzarne' (lynx) headed up the procession; he was followed by a 'London' pageant peopled with child actors (quite probably from the Merchant Taylors' School) depicting honourable qualities such as 'Magnanimity' as well as the Thames and the stock characters of 'The Souldier' and 'The Sayler'. Four nymphs brought the proceedings to a close with an encomium emphasizing virtue's worthiness and the desired state of peace and quietness for the City.

A few years later Peele was back in the frame. Again we find only one pageant device on display, but the book did introduce the innovation of a thematic title, *Descensus Astraeae*, a trend which was picked up again in the early 17th century. The introductory speech also struck the historical note that was to become the norm. Like the 1585 Show with its nymphs, the 1591 production had a pastoral air with the figure of Astrea and her 'sheephook' surmounting the pageant. Unlike in the later Shows, however, direct reference to the Lord Mayor himself was confined to the speech delivered as he travelled by water to Westminster to make his oath, where he was exhorted to 'Labour ... as other Maiors of yore / To beautifie the citie with desertes'. The post-Elizabethan Shows were to have a stronger take on individual Lord Mayors and their Companies and a deeper involvement in contemporary politics than their predecessors.

· SPEECHWRITERS IN THE EARLY MODERN PERIOD ·

· TRACEY HILL ·

PLANNING THE LOOK AND CONTENT OF the Lord Mayor's Show in the early modern period was a complex, expensive business. Speechwriters collaborated with 'artificers' who were responsible for physically creating the spectacle that characterized the day. The heyday of the early modern Show coincided with that of the stage, and many dramatists were employed to devise pageants, speeches and songs. George Peele, Thomas Middleton, Thomas Dekker, Anthony Munday, Thomas Heywood and John Webster – all better known now for their playwriting –

co-produced Shows in this period, as did the 'water poet' John Taylor. (Ben Jonson submitted an unsuccessful 'pitch' for the 1604 Show but then turned his attentions to the court masque.)

Of these, Munday, Middleton, Dekker and Heywood were the most ubiquitous. Munday dominated the Shows from the beginning of the 17th century until around 1618, when Middleton started to take over; Heywood was the main man from 1631 up to 1639, when the Show proper ceased as civil war loomed. Dekker had a hand in four Shows (1612, 1627, 1628 and 1629), and doubtless would have been involved in more had he not spent the intervening years in debtors' prison. Some of the writers were themselves freemen of the City of London: Munday was a Draper and Dekker a Merchant Taylor, and from 1620 until his death in 1627 Middleton held the important post of City Chronologer.

Often these writers and artificers vied for the lucrative and prestigious commission for the Show: the livery companies tried to haggle the fee down whilst the would-be production team, naturally, wanted the highest fee possible. In 1619, for example, the Skinners' Company recorded that 'Anthonie Mondaie, Thomas Middleton and Richard Grimston poetts, all shewed

LEFT: An 18th-century copperplate engraving of Thomas Middleton.

BELOW: An ostrich carved for Thomas Dekker's 'Londons Tempe' pageant of 1629, held at Ironmongers' Hall.

Vera Effigies
Tho. Midletoni Gent.

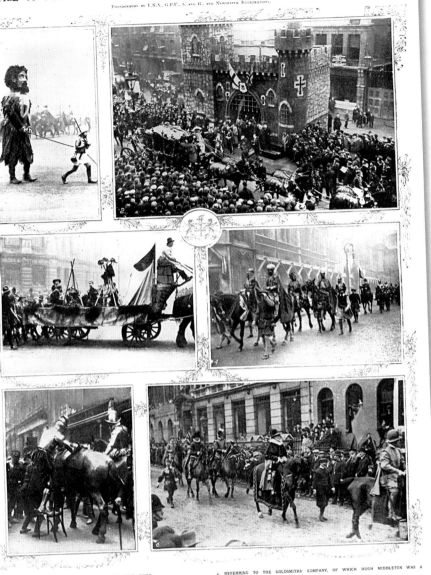

LED CAPTIVE BY THE GENIUS OF LONDON: THE NEW RIVER.

BEFORE A REPRODUCTION OF A FORMER KEY TO THE CITY: THE PRESENTATION OF AN ADDRESS TO THE LORD MAYOR OUTSIDE THE MODEL OF BAYNARD CASTLE.

INEVITABLE! A BOY SCOUTS' CAMP ON A TROLLEY.

4. REFERRING TO THE GOLDSMITHS' COMPANY, OF WHICH HUGH MIDDLETON WAS A MEMBER: "MOORISH KINGS."

5. MOUNTING HIS CHARGER WITH THE AID OF A CHAIR! A KNIGHT FOR THE PROCESSION.

6. COMPLETER AND INAUGURATOR OF THE NEW RIVER WATER-WORKS: HUGH MIDDLETON.

We are continually hearing that that most typical of London pageants, the Lord Mayor's Show, is a thing dead; yet every November it turns up again and draws great crowds to see it. This year's Procession proved no exception to the rule. As a special feature, had a Pageant which was an abridged reproduction of the Lord Mayor's Show of 1613, from the contemporary account written by Thomas Middleton, the dramatist, a namesake of the Lord Mayor of the time. In this Procession was Hugh Middleton, brother of the Lord Mayor of the year, who completed and inaugurated the New River water-works

on Michaelmas Day, 1613. Special interest attaches to the small reproduction of Baynard Castle set up at the corner of Queen Victoria Street and Upper Thames Street; for the new Lord Mayor's ward is Castle Baynard. The original Baynard Castle, which overlooked the river, took its name from Ralph Bainard, a follower of William the Conqueror. The first castle, destroyed by King John, was regarded as the key to the City, in whose first wall it was. A second Baynard's Castle, built by Humphrey, Duke of Gloucester, was practically destroyed by the Great Fire. Up to 1720 one tower remained.

LEFT: The 1913 Show – here reported by *The Illustrated London News* – was an abridged reproduction of Thomas Middleton's Show of 1613.

were undercut, though, for Thomas Heywood and his artificer John Christmas stepped in with 'their Invenc[i]on of 5 pageantes for the said shewe ... which Pageantes they offered to make furnish well & sufficiently ... for 180ˡⁱ [£180]'. That £10 saving made all the difference to the Ironmongers' Company, and they gave the job to Heywood and Christmas.

This is not to say that the City Companies were parsimonious. Writers and artificers were expected to use all their creative skills to produce lavish entertainments befitting the importance of the mayoral inauguration. Between five to seven pageant devices was the norm, and the content was tailored to fit both the Company and Lord Mayor in question. To give a flavour: for the 1629 Show Dekker and Christmas devised pageant devices for James Campbell, an Ironmonger. Scenes designed with 'much care, cost and curiosity', according to the printed book *Londons Tempe*, included Vulcan the mythical blacksmith in his forge, an ostrich (one of the Ironmongers' heraldic beasts), and 'The Field of Happiness', the name of which puns on 'Campbell'. The water show featured more legendary figures: Oceanus, King of the Sea, and his wife Tethys, seated on a sea-lion.

Such devices were accompanied by theatrical speeches, full of historical and mythical allusions, welcoming the new Lord Mayor to his domain. Word and act went hand in hand as the speechwriters and their collaborators pulled out all the stops to celebrate the power and antiquity of the City and its officers.

---

to the table their severall plotts for devices for the shewes and pagentes ... and each desired to serve the Companie'. Middleton won that commission.

One can see the negotiations in action over the 1635 Show for Christopher Clitheroe. Robert Norman (the artificer) and John Taylor (the writer) presented their 'project of 5 pageantes for the Lord Maiors shewe for which they demanded 190ˡⁱ [£190]', stating that 'under that price they would not undertake it'. They

· THE 1616 SHOW ·

· TRACEY HILL ·

THE SHOW FOR 1616 HELD TO CELEBRATE the inauguration of John Leman of the Fishmongers' Company is a special case due to the fortunate survival of a number of contemporary images of the pageantry of the day. Pictorial representations of mayoral pageantry from this period are rare indeed, and the Fishmongers' drawings bring to life the devices described in Anthony Munday's pageant book, *Chrysanaleia*.

Munday was a very experienced hand, having by then already co-produced at least six and possibly as many as ten Lord Mayor's Shows. The Fishmongers' Company, in contrast, had not had the privilege of a Lord Mayor from their ranks for over 25 years, which might explain what doubtless would have been the expensive commission of this series of drawings, not to mention the expenditure on the actual Show. The latter comprised the conventional combination of emblematic devices based on topics and figures relevant to the Company, linked together with a characteristically Munday-esque emphasis on their historical significance.

Chrysanaleia, however, began with an atypically personal note. Probably already at work on his 1618 continuation and enlargement of John Stow's magisterial *Survey of London*, Munday took a moment to reflect on his relationship with the City and with the Company who sponsored the Show. Being an 'Orphan childe' whose care had been given over to the City at a young age, he noted the 'Patronage and protection' and the 'favour and kinde cherishing' he had received

BELOW: The King of the Moors, in an 1844 illustration copied from the Fishmongers' *Chrysanaleia* pageant scroll of 1616.

ABOVE: The King of the Moors in the original 1616 pageant scroll.

ABOVE: The 'Chariot
of Triumphall Victory',
the final float in the
1616 pageant.

one of the central images of the Show around Leman's
role, utilizing the emblem of 'the pelican in her piety',
combined with a pun, 'lemon', on his name, to
demonstrate the Mayor's selfless governance.

Naturally, the Fishmongers' Company had an equal
significance in the Show. The procession began with
a 'fishing Busse, called the Fishmongers Esperanza,
or Hope of London', which featured in performance
some small child actors throwing fish to the watching
crowds. The piscine theme continued into the next
device, a 'crowned Dolphin' that referred to both the
Fishmongers' coat of arms and also to those of Leman.
One of the most striking images of the Show must
have been the 'King of Moores, mounted on a golden
Leopard ... hurling gold and silver euery way about
him', as one can see from the relevant drawing; this
device alluded to the longstanding 'amity' between
the Fishmongers and the Goldsmiths.

But the conceptual heart of the Show returned to the
history of Leman's Company. Munday and Grinkin
had designed a 'bower', in which lay one of the
Fishmongers' greatest heroes, William Walworth (*see
page 10*). Walworth was celebrated in London for his
role in the 1381 Peasants' Revolt, where according to
legend he slew the ringleader, Wat Tyler, at Smithfield
in front of King Richard II. This deed was, naturally,
incorporated into the pageantry: 'London's Genius' sat
on horseback by the bower bearing Tyler's dissevered
head on Walworth's dagger. The act of this famed
Lord Mayor ensured, the text proclaimed, 'the
Fishmongers Fame foreuer', and so it was fitting that
the Show should conclude with a pageant chariot on
which the 'triumphing' angel who 'smote the enemy
by Walworths hand' sat in precedence to an array of
'Royall Vertues' and even to King Richard himself.

(and which, he implied, he hoped would continue). John
Leman's personal circumstances were also accentuated
in the book. Munday foregrounded the fact that
Leman, unusually for a Lord Mayor, was unmarried,
in order to highlight the ways in which the City's
chief magistrate would for his term of office act as a
husband as well as a 'nursing father' to the metropolis.
Indeed, Munday and the artificer John Grinkin built

RIGHT: A portrait of Sir
John Leman from 1616.

· THE PORTRAIT OF SIR JOHN ROBINSON ·

· MARTIN GAYFORD ·

ON 17 MARCH 1663 THE DIARIST SAMUEL
Pepys was 'up betimes', spent the day attending various
court cases and ended it drinking in a cellar under the
Tower of London. His companions in this carousal
were Sir Richard Ford MP and the Lord Mayor of
London, Sir John Robinson. Before going to bed, Pepys
confided his opinion of the two men to his diary: Ford
he thought 'a very able man of his brains and tongue'.
But, after 'many discourses', and drinking ('which as
always going on'), he found Robinson to be 'a talking,
bragging Bufflehead'.

This is the man depicted in a portrait by John Michael
Wright a year earlier, in 1662. This picture could almost
serve as an illustration to Pepys' night out – Wright has
a reputation for realism, as well as an ability to convey
baroque splendour. In the background of the painting
is the Tower. Robinson, who was then its Lieutenant,
languidly indicates the White Tower through the
window with a gesture that also encompasses the
Lord Mayor's robes and chain of office lying on the
table beside him. At the age of 47 he looks very pleased
with himself, just as Pepys noted in November 1665
on another occasion when Robinson drank too much.
Pepys recorded his merriment that Robinson made it
'his work to praise himself and all he says and doth –
like a heavy-headed coxcomb'. The paunch which can
be seen in Wright's portrait discreetly swelling beneath
the honorific breastplate (he took no part in military
engagement) testifies to the 'strange pleasure' Pepys

felt Robinson and his companions took in their 'wine
and meat', together with their tendency to discuss
it with a 'curiosity and joy' beneath men of such
rank. This last point makes Robinson, the garrulous
gourmet, sound a rather sympathetic figure.

Others were more complimentary about the Lord
Mayor. The Venetian ambassador, for example,
described him as 'a rich and talented man'. And if he
appeared self-satisfied in the early 1660s, he had plenty
of reason, for he had just played a role in the most
important political event of the age: the Restoration of
the Stuart monarchy. On 8 May 1660 parliament had
proclaimed Charles II as king. Robinson was not only
a member of parliament but also regarded as the 'leader'
of the City of London. Charles was grateful for his
support. Three days before the king entered the City on
29 May, Robinson was knighted. The following month
he was created a baronet, and the same year he became
Lieutenant of the Tower of London.

Robinson had thus not only done very well for himself
but he had also assisted a cause in which he strongly
believed. He came from a family that was at once
ecclesiastical and mercantile. His grandfather was a
successful clothier from Reading, and his father was an
archdeacon in the Church of England and half-brother
of William Laud, Archbishop of Canterbury under
Charles I. This made Robinson at once wealthy,
High Church to the point of favouring Catholicism

and a fervent supporter of the monarchy. He was
thought to be 'as great a Cavalier as was in England':
that is, no one was more pro-Stuart than he.

The Lord Mayor considered himself, no doubt, a great
merchant and aristocrat, able to swing opinion in
London. He was valued as such by the king and the
court. Wright may well have had some fellow feeling

for Robinson. Born in 1617, the two men were almost
the same age. The painter was a Catholic convert; the
Lord Mayor was a High Church Anglican suspected
of sympathy for Catholicism. Both men curried favour
at court. Nonetheless, amply though Wright's portrait
reflects the subject's dignity, success and grandeur, you
can't help feeling there is a glimpse too of the 'bragging
Bufflehead' Pepys so rudely described.

❶ · PLAGUE, STORMS AND THE GREAT FIRE ·

· TRACEY HILL ·

FOR THE MOST PART, THE EARLY MODERN Lord Mayor's Show was a splendid event as was befitting the importance of the role it inaugurated. Sometimes, however, external events had a calamitous impact on the planned festivities. On at least one occasion the Show was curtailed simply because of the weather, a constant threat in late October. In 1605 the entire Show was repeated on All Saints Day in November due to the 'very wett and fowle weather' of the original date. Additional expenses included 'repayring the Pageant, and the rest of the other shewes', re-buying the apparel for the child actors, purchasing coal for fires to dry out the pageants, and so on.

More significant and better-known events were, of course, the Great Plague of 1665 and the Great Fire of the following year, both of which are explored below. 1665 was by no means the only year when the Show was affected by an outbreak of plague, something the City was subjected to on an almost annual basis. Twice in the 17th century, by some strange coincidence, London experienced at the same moment the consequences of both plague and the death of a monarch. There was no full-scale Show with all the usual street pageantry in 1603, when Elizabeth I died, nor in 1625, which saw the death of James I. Both years were also marked by particularly bad plague outbreaks, with many thousands dying. It was hardly appropriate – even if the relevant personnel had survived – for the City to be seen to be 'en fête' in the face of such a widespread trauma. Thomas

Middleton commented in the 1626 Show that 'Tryumph was not ... in season' in 1625, a year when 'Deaths Pageants' displaced celebratory pageants. The 1626 Show emphasized the hardship of a time when 'a cloude of griefe hath showrde vpon the face / Of this sad City, and vsurpt the place / Of Ioy and Cheerfulnesse'.

The cataclysm of 1665/6 exceeded all these previous instances. First, the City was visited with one of the worst episodes of plague it had faced to date, and then,

in early September 1666, the Great Fire took hold, only six weeks before the date of the Show. Naturally, nothing along the lines of the usual extraordinary spectacle was possible on either occasion. In 1666, while the City's ashes still smouldered, a much reduced inauguration took place: the water show on the Thames and other pageantry was omitted, and Sir William Bolton, the new Lord Mayor, simply rode in his coach to Westminster, accompanied by the Aldermen, Sheriffs and 'several eminent Citizens'. It took a long while for the City to return to normal: in 1667 the Merchant Taylors' Company account books contain just a poignant list of 'nil' payments for the usual mayoral expenses; even in 1668 they struggled to produce the traditional festivities and were forced to hold the dinner to mark the inauguration of their member William Turner in improvised sheds.

Worse still, the 1666 Lord Mayor, William Bolton, let the City down in many ways. He refused to accept a reduced sum for the conventional 'beautifieing of his howse', despite the parlous conditions of the time, and disgraced himself further by embezzling £1,800 of donations intended for poor victims of the Fire, 'of which he can give no account, and in which he hath forsworn himself plainly', according to Samuel Pepys. Fortunately, these travails were infrequent, and when disaster did strike, the livery companies did their best to retain at least the formalities of the mayoral inauguration, even when the glitzy extravagance of other years proved impossible to pull off.

· RIOTS IN 1830 ·

· BRIAN MAIDMENT ·

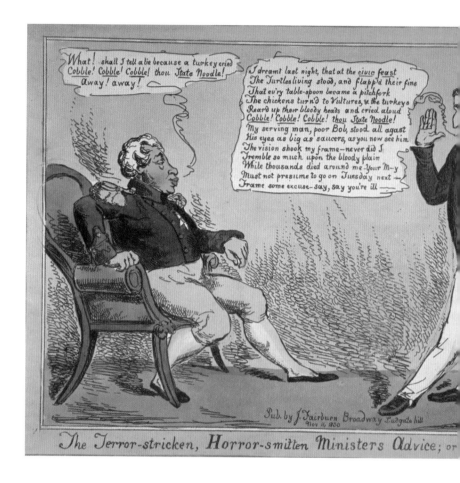

THE PARTIAL CANCELLATION OF THE
Lord Mayor's Show in November 1830, an occasion
that was to have been graced by the presence of
William IV, constituted a disastrous moment in the
already highly compromised career of the Prime
Minister, the Duke of Wellington. The previous
few years had seen the Tory government of Peel and
Wellington forcing unpopular measures through
parliament but at the same time resisting others that
had been demanded by popular opinion as well as
opposition politicians. The Catholic Emancipation
Act of 1829, which had admitted Catholic MPs to full
membership of parliament, had been passed in spite of
widespread opposition. The long and highly charged
debate over the need for parliamentary reform, which
eventually led to the Reform Act of 1832, seethed
on, however, and on the recall of parliament on
2 November 1830, a week before the Lord Mayor's
Show was due to take place, Wellington had made
an outspoken and intransigent speech against any
changes to the electoral system in the face of the
carefully moderate views of opposition MPs such as
Lord Grey. Wellington's position had been further
weakened by the death of Huskisson, run down by
a locomotive on the Liverpool and Manchester
railway during a government visit to northern
industrial towns. The economic situation of the
country was also dire, with frequent mass protests
about the state of the nation unhappily recalling
the Peterloo Massacre of 1819.

In these circumstances it is hardly surprising that
Wellington would have feared for his safety and that
of the king were they to appear as planned in the Lord
Mayor's Show. On Saturday 6 November the Lord
Mayor-Elect, Sir John Key, wrote to Peel and Wellington
asking for the deployment of a large military force
to protect the dignitaries. Peel, as Home Secretary,
had received many written threats, and the king had
already written to Wellington to suggest postponing his
presence in the City. An anonymous etching published
by John Fairburn shows Wellington, accompanied by
Peel, asking the king to postpone his visit (*above*). Even
given the considerable damage to an already highly
unpopular administration, it was agreed that neither the
king nor Wellington should attend the Lord Mayor's
Show. Highly policed celebrations still went ahead,
however, including a rally of radicals in the Blackfriars

ABOVE: Wellington
recounts a dream he has
had of impending disaster.
The king here refuses
his minister's advice and
remains set on attending
the Lord Mayor's Show,
suggesting, in this distortion
of the facts, the extent to
which Wellington had
fallen victim to his
own unpopularity.

l Visit postponed

Rotunda, and a street presence of over 30,000 people, 600 of whom advanced on Downing Street. But major trouble was avoided, and a lower police and military presence managed to deal with lesser gatherings on 8 and 9 November. Wellington had barricaded himself into Apsley House, and the immediate crisis receded.

However bad the events of 1830 might have been for Wellington, they proved a wonderful opportunity for caricaturists to show that they had lost none of the energy and vitality of the more famous previous generation of graphic satirists such as Gillray and Rowlandson. By 1830 the etched and engraved single plate political caricature was beginning to be overtaken in popularity by more diversionary, less acerbic sociopolitical comic publications. Nonetheless particular political events proved irresistible to caricaturists, and Wellington's brand of contempt for popular opinion had made him a repeated target for trenchant graphic satires. The misdeeds of London dignitaries, too, were a traditional topic. The indulgences of previous Lord Mayors frequently formed the subject of caricatures. An 1824 caricature by William Heath for instance had offered damning commentary on a famously indulgent Lord Mayor, Sir William Curtis, under the magnificent title of 'The patent stomach reliever or extracting superfluities, excesses & all sorts of poisons', a print that showed, amongst much other evidence of greed, an Alderman stuffing whole chicken legs into his mouth. Drawing on this tradition of popular hostility to previous Lord Mayors, the wave of prints from 1830 frequently described their excesses, suggesting that the visual memory of the populace was both capacious and unforgiving. Such traditional hostility to Lord Mayors, if not to the

theatrical pleasures of their annual Shows, also appears in caricatures centrally concerned with the particular political events of 1830, freighting the images with a remembered hostility to civic indulgences past and present.

Not only Wellington stood accused of cowardice in the face of the angry populace. Another anonymous etching shows the Lord Mayor-Elect surrounded by various City figures, including a pupil of Christ's Hospital, as one in their collective fear of the consequences of allowing the Lord Mayor's Show to go ahead (*below*). Clearly the artist thinks they are a sorry lot. Caricatures such as these suggest that, if the political unpopularity of Wellington remained the major impulse for satire and abuse, there was also apparent a long-standing dissatisfaction with the privileges, excesses and contempt of the City dignitaries for the mass of the people. Graphic satire, formulated in the traditional forms and gestural language of the caricature tradition, remained a major force in amusing its audience and in both guiding and reflecting popular indignation.

RIGHT: Clutching various emblems of their privileges and standing in front of posters that describe the potential overthrow of traditional City habits, the assembled dignitaries exhibit both fear and disapproval.

· THE 1915 SHOW ·

· JOHN DAVIS ·

ONLY ANTIQUARIANS AMONGST THE crowds watching the Lord Mayor's Show on 9 November 1915 would have been aware of the 700th anniversary of the Mayoral Charter. Fifteen months into the First World War, the City of London Corporation had acceded to the War Office's request to use the event as a recruiting exercise, dispelling any temptation to celebrate the City's past. Aside from its instinctive patriotic support for the war effort, the Corporation valued the political advantage of putting the Show to public use. Popular as the usual pageant was, it was depicted by the City's opponents as an exercise in civic flummery, advertising the Corporation's unreformed status. By devoting the Show to the war effort, the City defused such criticism: 'The pageant has had its critics in the past', wrote the *City Press* correspondent, 'this year it has not a single one.'

For the military authorities the context was critical. The rush to the colours evident in the early months of the war had subsided and, with heavy casualties on the Western Front, the British Army needed men by the autumn of 1915. The contentious option of military conscription divided the coalition government, which instead introduced a compromise scheme in October 1915 inviting men of military age to 'attest' their willingness to serve if required. The purpose of the 1915 Show was to encourage men to attest.

ABOVE: Members of the Women's Land Army participating in the Show during the First World War.

LEFT: An RAF float displaying aircraft guns and bombs, 9 November 1918.

THE ROYAL NAVAL AIR SERVICE IN THE LORD MAYOR'S SHOW: ONE OF THE ANTI-AIRCRAFT GUNS AND A SEARCHLIGHT IN THE PROCESSION.

WITH ITS WINGS "CLIPPED," THAT IT MIGHT BE DRAWN THROUGH THE STREETS: AN AEROPLANE OF THE R.F.C.

CAPTURED AT LOOS: ENEMY GUNS DRAWN THROUGH THE STREETS OF LONDON AS PART OF THE LORD MAYOR'S SHOW.

H CHEERED BY THE ONLOOKERS: THE "ANZAC" (AUSTRALIAN AND NEW ZEALAND) CONTINGENT.

A VERY POPULAR FEATURE: CANADIAN HIGHLANDERS MARCHING IN THE LORD MAYOR'S PROCESSION.

Lord Mayor's Show of this, the second year of the Great War, took exceptional ppropriate form, and was very successful despite the bad weather. It started at from the Guildhall, earlier than usual because it was arranged that the Guildhall et in the evening should begin at six o'clock instead of the customary seven. ed in the Procession were some German guns captured by our forces; a detachment Anti-aircraft Corps, with guns; a detachment of the R.F.C., with aeroplane; a ment of the City of London National Guard; a Canadian Contingent; and Con-

tingents representing Australia and New Zealand, South Africa, and the West Indies. In addition were representatives of various regiments, the Royal Naval Division, the Royal Marine Artillery, and the Royal Marine Light Infantry. Other very prominent features were recruiting bands and, following the Lord Mayor and his escort of City of London Yeomanry, a Recruiting Column of considerable strength. Before the arrival of the Procession, recruiting meetings were held at various points of the route, and it was arranged that recruits should fall in in rear of the Guards detachment.

ABOVE: A page from *The Illustrated London News*, 13 November 1915.

Recruiting meetings were held at ten points along the procession's route, addressed by MPs and army men; those attesting could participate in the parade. The procession was unambiguously military. The Lord Mayor's coach was preceded by anti-aircraft guns, parts of a military biplane, a requisitioned omnibus labelled 'Reinforcements', captured German guns, Red Cross ambulances and 'a long string of ammunition and supply wagons'. The parade comprised 'soldiers – soldiers all the way', as the *City Press* put it, including many

'direct from the trenches' ('Yesterday they were facing death at any moment; today they were ... luxuriating in the cheers of tens of thousands of Londoners.') Servicemen from the Dominions participated, *The Times* noting the 'finely built men with alert bronzed faces' from Australia and New Zealand. A West Indian company received 'a specially hearty cheer'. The parade – a mile and a half long – involved 5,000 people.

All found it impressive. The *City Press* correspondent declared that only the 'veriest slacker' would not be stirred by such a display, but its success as a recruiting exercise remains unclear. Abysmal weather, varying from drizzle to downpour, deterred men from hearing recruiting speeches lasting 'thirty or thirty-five minutes'. At the Royal Exchange, Major Rigg's warning of 'the march of German soldiery into the City' should the war be lost chilled a crowd 'only of moderate dimensions'. At St Paul's station (present-day Blackfriars) listeners 'preferred to remain under the shelter of the railway bridge nearby, and were not beguiled therefrom by the eloquence of the recruiting speakers.' The recruiters were, after all, appealing to men who had resisted early public enthusiasm for the war, and who by November 1915 harboured few illusions about trench warfare. *The Times'* lyrical account of the rain-soaked procession – of 'rusting bayonets and lances, khaki uniforms stained by the downpour to the colour of wet mud', which 'brought to the mind stories of grim days in France and Flanders and visions of the things which must happen before there can be peace again' – was convincing but hardly enticing. By November 1916 conscription had been introduced, making recruitment stunts of this nature redundant. The 1915 Lord Mayor's Show was the first and last of its kind.

THE SHOW IN THE 1940s ·

· JOHN DAVIS ·

IN NOVEMBER 1939, THE *CITY PRESS* noted, 'there was no Lord Mayor's Show in the sense of a pageant.' The formalities of the change of Mayoralty were observed, and a procession of sorts took place, but it was 'shorn of much of its picturesque charm', lacking 'the semi-State Coach, with its fine horses ... the State Trumpeters, and, last but not least ... the City Marshal, whose cocked hat and feathers were sadly missed.' The Lord Mayor and other dignitaries processed in private cars. While the 'phoney war' continued, many questioned this asceticism. 'Patriotism demands that we all acquiesce in having nothing worth looking at by day and no light to see anything with at night', complained *The Times'* correspondent, who envisaged a puritanical wartime Show in which the Lord Mayor 'would be driven to a selected air-raid shelter where he would be received by the Controller of Turtle Soup and his staff'.

By Lord Mayor's Day in 1941, such sarcasm appeared misplaced. Diners at the Mansion House luncheon (which had replaced the traditional Guildhall banquet) were assured that 'in the event of it becoming necessary to vacate the Hall, Guests will be conducted to shelter accommodation.' Though the previous Lord Mayor referred to 'the awful carnage and destruction in cities like Warsaw, Rotterdam and Belgrade', the bomb damage in the City itself was evident enough. *The Times* noted that that year's procession was headed by the Civil Defence Services, who, traversing the City, passed 'many a desolate reminder of their own heroic struggle in the worst hours of London's air raids.'

By then the spartan pattern of wartime parades was established: 'motor cars took the place of horses, and even cars were used sparingly'; 'a brisk and efficient

ABOVE: Herbert Mason's iconic photograph of St Paul's Cathedral during the Blitz, 29/30 December 1940.

INSET: Lord Mayor Sir John Laurie greets Winston Churchill at Mansion House prior to the Banquet in 1941.

ABOVE: Australian
soldiers marching
through the heart of
the bombed-out City
during the 1941 Show.

RIGHT: A Vickers-
Armstrong Valentine tank,
one of many taking part
in the 1941 Show.

their motor-bicycles in the van of a sombre string of motor-cars.... Even more grim was the escort of six self-propelled anti-aircraft guns manned by their steel-helmeted crews.' It was reported that after exchanging the insignia of office at Guildhall, the new and old Lord Mayors left to an amplified recording of Bow Bells, the real bells being 'broken and down'. This ersatz performance was repeated in 1944, the *City Press* noting balefully that the bells of St Mary-le-Bow 'will not ring again until the Church is rebuilt after the war.'

The underlying optimism regarding the war's outcome was warranted, but even in 1945, six months after VE Day, the coach remained unused for want of horses to pull it. Only in 1946 did the Lord Mayor and Sheriffs' Committee decide to 'revive what is popularly known as the Lord Mayor's Show', at a cost of £4,000. The peacetime pageant, featuring worthy themes such as agriculture in 1947 and transport in 1949, returned gradually, but the City of London Corporation could not ignore postwar austerity, replacing the wartime Mansion House luncheon by 'a Dinner (not a Banquet)' at Guildhall from 1946. Only the Lord Mayor-Elect's diffident request, in that year, that 'there should be something such as a Lobster Patty in place of Soup at the dinner' promised a more opulent future.

parade' of British and Dominion troops, accompanied by 'Allied and Associated Forces' from the Free French and occupied Belgium, Czechoslovakia, the Netherlands, Norway and Poland, replaced the peacetime pageant. Spectators were sparse, deterred by 'curtailed train and bus services and the more general injunction to travel only when necessary.' The absence of flowers at the Mansion House luncheon was remarked upon in 1942. In 1943, after years of stoicism, *The Times*' correspondent lost patience, decrying the 'grim, mechanized procession – perhaps the shortest ever seen on a ninth of November. Military dispatch riders in crash helmets rode

CANALETTO'S *WESTMINSTER BRIDGE FROM THE NORTH WITH THE LORD MAYOR'S PROCESSION, 29 OCTOBER 1746* ·

· ANDREW GRAHAM-DIXON ·

ON 29 OCTOBER 1746 THE NEW LORD MAYOR of London, William Benn of the Fletchers' Company, was carried by barge from the City to Westminster to swear the customary oath, as long-established ceremony demanded. The barge he sat in was burnished with gold, or at least generously decorated with gold-leaf, and vividly adorned with statues of gilded oak. One pennant fluttered from the prow, another from the stern, and four more from poles placed at the corners of the state cabin: a structure occupying fully half the length of the boat, supported on Corinthian columns, designed to protect its illustrious occupant and his retinue from the likely inclemency of English weather in the autumn.

The Lord Mayor's barge was rowed by a team of oarsman in crisp white shirts and bright red trousers, drawn from the Company of Watermen and Lightermen. It was accompanied by a flotilla of other, only slightly less splendidly decked-out ceremonial barges belonging to the City livery companies: the Skinners, the Goldsmiths, the Fishmongers; the Clothworkers, the Vintners, the Merchant Taylors; the Mercers and the Drapers. A host of other, smaller boats joined in the procession, most of them vessels for gawkers and gapers wanting to take as close a part as possible in 18th-century London's most spectacular public pageant. Thousands more onlookers thronged the banks of the Thames to watch the grand show float past.

A painter was among their number: Giovanni Antonio Canal, commonly known as Canaletto, an Italian recently arrived in the English capital from his native city

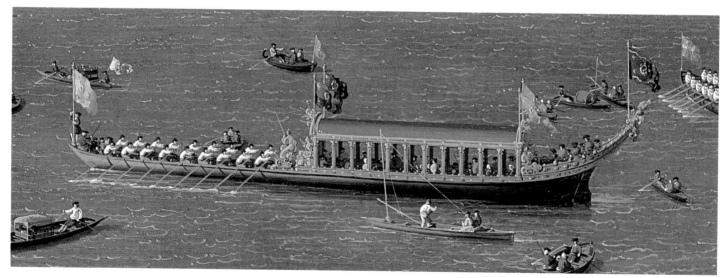

of Venice. George Vertue, an invaluable source of gossip about the art and artists of the time, noted Canaletto's arrival in one of the pages of his journal for 1746: 'Latter end of May came to London from Venice the Famous Painter of Views Cannaletti [sic] ... of Venice, the Multitude of his works done abroad for English noblemen & Gentlemen has procured him great reputation & his great merrit & excellence in that way, he is much esteemed and no doubt but what Views and works He doth here, will give the same satisfaction – though many persons already have so many of his paintings.'

Canaletto's splendid panorama of a painting, *Westminster Bridge from the North with the Lord Mayor's Procession, 29 October 1746*, may have been created, in part, to draw attention to his presence in England: an advertisement of his considerable skills, intended to drum up new business among the picture-buying elite of London. Business had certainly not been going so well for Canaletto in Venice, where he had previously specialized in painting and selling pictures of the world's most picturesque city – with its Rialto Bridge, its Grand Canal and its multitude of softly mouldering palaces – to English milords and other tourists in search of souvenirs. Thanks to the War of the Austrian Succession, few foreigners were making the trip to Venice any more, and the demand for his work had all but dried up. Travelling to London, the largest city in Europe, busy hub of a thriving, thrusting, expanding imperial power, he hoped to revive his fortunes.

In choosing to paint the Lord Mayor's Show, Canaletto probably had his eye not just on prospective aristocratic patrons but also the lucrative market for popular prints in London. After all, this was one of the most popular festivals in the annual calendar, so a mass-produced image

of it might well be sold profitably to the public at large (and indeed a print was made after Canaletto's painting, although how much he gained from it is not known). In choosing to paint the procession at the moment of its impending arrival at Westminster Bridge, he was consciously adding a degree of spice and controversy to his depiction of the event. The bridge was a new landmark at the time, still not quite complete, and its construction had been bedevilled by opposition and criticism, most notably from London's famously vociferous watermen, the taxi-drivers of the day, all 30,000 of whom felt their livelihood to be endangered by such an evident convenience to pedestrian and horse-drawn traffic. Canaletto presented the structure as a gleaming miracle of modern engineering,

a symbol of London's grand stature as the new capital city of Europe. In fact he made it even more perfect than it yet was, or ever would be, by including at its centre a pair of statues personifying the ancient goddess Isis and the River Thames. These were planned, in his time, but had not yet been added to the bridge. In the end, they never were.

Canaletto departed from the truth in other ways too, principally by bathing the scene in distinctly Venetian sunshine and omitting the pall of smoke that always hung over the Thames back in those days. This has sometimes been said to prove that he was unequipped to paint the rainsqualls and persistent smog of early industrial London. But it may well have been intentional, and meaningful. The Whig aristocrats of Georgian England, who were the painter's main patrons, often expressed a deep sympathy for the republican political structure of the Venetian republic. So it is possible that Canaletto made London look rather like Venice in order to echo that sense of fellow feeling. Whatever the precise motives behind the painting, it remains a glitteringly beautiful perpetuation of a moment from the vanished past.

There are still echoes of the old waterborne Lord Mayor's Shows in the modern world. Even now, as the Lord Mayor processes to Westminster by land rather than water, he is accompanied by liveried watermen carrying admittedly obsolete oars. Even now, whenever anyone uses the word 'float' in the context of a festival procession, they are, whether knowingly or not, using a term that has its origins in the original floating festival that was the Lord Mayor's Show. But the only way to bring that festival before your eyes, in all its colour and pageantry, is to look at Canaletto's painting.

· ANDREW GRAHAM-DIXON ·

HAVING COMPLETED THE FIRST PART of his procession along the Thames by boat, Francis Goodchild rides in a horsedrawn coach towards Guildhall to be inaugurated Lord Mayor of London. Visible only as a sliver of self-congratulatory profile amid a sea of jostling onlookers, he makes his way through crowded streets under the impassive gaze of Frederick, Prince of Wales and his consort Princess Augusta, who look on from a balcony above the throng.

The Lord Mayor is accompanied by dignitaries, one of whom solemnly brandishes the Sword of State at the coach window. Four lackeys cling precariously to the back of the carriage, tugged backwards as if by a strong wind, while a great London crowd surges around them. Temporary stands have been set up for the occasion. These constructions of wood and canvas are filled with variously drunken, disorderly, and lecherous revellers, including a couple snogging with such fierce abandon they seem about to topple from their perch. Nearby, some ragtag militiamen are drinking beer by the mugful. One or two of them are accidentally discharging their muskets in the general direction of a row of houses opposite. At their windows stand more spectators, apparently oblivious to the threat of stray grapeshot. There is festivity in the air, but also a sense that things could soon turn ugly, and that the celebrations might boil over into a riot.

Francis Goodchild never did become Lord Mayor of London, for the simple reason that he was a fictitious character. William Hogarth invented him, and launched him on the world, with careful timing, on 17 October 1747, less than two weeks before the day of the real Lord Mayor's Show (an event commemorated that same year by Hogarth's contemporary, the Italian painter Canaletto). The *London Evening Post* carried Hogarth's advertisment: '*This Day is publish'd,*

BELOW: Detail from *The Idle 'Prentice Executed at Tyburn*, plate 11 of *Industry and Idleness*, 1747.

Price 12s, Designed and Engraved by Mr Hogarth. TWELVE Prints, call'd INDUSTRY and IDLENESS: Shewing the Advantages attending the former, and the miserable Effects of the latter, in the different Fortunes of two APPRENTICES.'

Hogarth's *Industry and Idleness* was a successor to his previous, highly successful series of prints telling the stories of ill-fated Londoners: *The Rake's Progress* and *The Harlot's Progress*. But whereas in the previous series Hogarth had grimly focused on vice, exposing the follies of a dissolute spendthrift and a fallen woman, now he introduced a measure of virtue, contrasting the sorry tale of another wastrel with the uplifting parable of a self-made man. Tom Idle, the Idle Apprentice, gets drunk and sleeps at his loom, gambles to the point of ruin, falls in with highwaymen and meets a sticky end. Francis Goodchild, the Industrious Apprentice, works hard, goes to church and receives his just rewards, marrying his master's daughter, taking over the business and eventually rising through the ranks of London's citizenry to become Alderman and, finally, Lord Mayor of London.

The Industrious 'Prentice Lord-Mayor of London is the last of the 12 plates of Hogarth's *Industry and Idleness*, and brings the series to its morally righteous climax. The humble former apprentice has become Lord Mayor of London; virtue has been resoundingly rewarded. It is immediately preceded in Hogarth's sequence by a print that looks, at first sight, quite similar. The pair to Francis Goodchild's apotheosis as Lord Mayor, it also represents a crowd scene, and also has at its focal point a figure processing on a horse-drawn carriage. But in that image Tom Idle is on an executioner's cart travelling to the gallows at Tyburn, attended not by dignitaries but by a fervent Methodist preacher exhorting him to repent of his sins.

Despite the apparent clarity of Hogarth's moral scheme, there is an ambiguity at the heart of *Industry and Idleness*, which may have stemmed from an ambiguity in Hogarth's sense of himself. There were close parallels between his own story and that of the Industrious Apprentice. He too had married the daughter of his master, James Thornhill, and taken over the business and prospered. When devising *Industry and Idleness* he even toyed with giving his virtuous character the name William Goodchild, rather than Francis, a decision which would have underscored the artist's self-identification with his hero. But he held back, perhaps because he knew that to do so would have been to tell a kind of lie about himself and the world in which he lived. There were equally strong links between Hogarth and the Idle Apprentice. In his writings he frequently berated himself for 'idleness', and seems often to have felt he was lucky to have achieved such success. Like Tom Idle, he never completed his apprenticeship, was prone to bouts of heavy drinking and sometimes disappeared for days at a time with his companions in debauchery.

Perhaps this helps to explain the disquieting mood of unruliness and uncertainty that hangs over Hogarth's vision of the Lord Mayor's Show. Not only is the joyful procession mirrored by its opposite, the grim approach to Tyburn, but one might become the other as easily as a crowd might become a mob. The tales of the two apprentices can be read as a single tale twisted in two different directions by a capricious fate. Fame and fortune were precariously attained in 18th-century London, as Hogarth well knew. A man could rise to the top of society or fall to the very bottom. There might seem to be a huge gulf between the Lord Mayor of London and a common criminal, but in reality the distance separating the two was, perhaps, not so great.

Designed by Wm Hogarth

Proverbs CHAP: III. V...

Length of days is in her right h...
in her left hand Riches and...

Plate 12.

Published by T. Cook, Islington, and G.G. & J. Robinsons Pater-nos...

LEFT: William Hogarth's
*The Industrious 'Prentice
Lord-Mayor of London.*

· LOGSDAIL'S *THE NINTH OF NOVEMBER, 1888* ·

· WILLIAM LOGSDAIL ·

THESE EXTRACTS ARE FROM WILLIAM Logsdail's own account of how he created his masterpiece *The Ninth of November, 1888*, which depicts the Lord Mayor's Show passing the Royal Exchange. Completed in 1890, the painting was bought by Sir James Whitehead, Lord Mayor in 1889, and acquired by the Guildhall Art Gallery in 1932.

'After about six years in Venice I had come to London, to try and paint scenes in London itself. Surely there is nothing in the whole world more worthy to be painted....

On 9th November 1887 I was led by fate to join the crowd and see the Lord Mayor's Show go by. As I watched the gorgeous old coach with its six horses in crimson harness, coachmen, postillion and footmen all laced in gold, and its escort of hussars go glittering and jangling through the gloom and grime – their finery shining like daffodils in contrast to the drab crowds huddled along the footway – here, I thought, is the chance for a big picture....

I became excited. When sufficiently so I never in any of my undertakings consider the cost in labour, time, outlay or any difficulties to be overcome. Nor did I consider whether the subject would sell, or the ultimate destination of the picture....

I at once ordered the biggest canvas that I had hitherto attempted and made sketches for the general arrangement. For my background I chose the very heart of things, where the Show is passing the Mansion House, showing the Bank and Royal Exchange.

Then followed a long time passed on the spot. First at daybreak, when the City is silent and empty, and I posed the solitary policeman on duty here and there to get the correct scale for my figures. Then many a long day spent between the columns of Mansion House, making large studies for my architectural background. This was an exhausting job in the midst of that terrible traffic, being before the days of motors and rubber wheels.

But that was play in comparison to the real difficulties to come. A large part of my time and energy was spent in getting together the material required. This was all painted from the actual thing or from life. The coach, horses, coachmen, postillion, footmen, hussars, foot and mounted police, and the varied types to form a London crowd – all had to be procured.

Through the kindness of Mr Soulsby ... Private Secretary at the Mansion House for many years, I got authority to go to the stables in Fore Street and have the coach drawn out whenever I wanted it, and the horses harnessed for my studies. He also had the Corporation mace got out for me to paint from.

The coachmen and footmen all brought their liveries to pose for me at my studio at Primrose Hill, where

ABOUT: Detail from William Logsdail's *The Ninth of November, 1888*, 1890.

minstrel, stealing apples from the basket just behind the policeman.

The Irish apple woman had a regular pitch for some years at the entrance to Regent's Park near the Zoo. While posing, she fell in a faint on the floor of my studio and I had to unfasten her frock and administer whiskey, which she refused to allow me to dilute.

For the burly policeman, I procured the uniform and put it on an old friend of mine, a landscape painter named P.M. Feeney.

The man with the white moustache and beard is Mills, the head of Newman's, the colourman in Soho Square. A good Samaritan to many a needy painter, who omitted to send in the bill for colours supplied.

J.W. Waterhouse, R.A. is in a brown bowler hat just behind the guardsman and his flapper.

Behind Waterhouse, in a top hat, is Douglas Adams, a landscape painter. Between the heads of the two footmen appears Wolfe in a Turkish tarbush, which he commonly wore when at Primrose Hill studios. The rest are all professional models or types picked up in the street.

I had had an additional glass studio erected to get an open air light on my models: a great expense in addition to the daily payment of models, tips, hire of horses etc.

Taking some of the principal figures from left to right: the minstrel was a professional model, who hired the costume for me. I asked if he knew a little guttersnipe of the pickpocket type.... he appears in front of the

Towards the end I began to have some hopes as to the result.... I also heard it said frequently that the picture should be bought for the Guildhall Art Gallery. I still think they will be glad to have it, for as every year goes by, it will be of increasing value for such a Gallery as an historical record of exactly how the Lord Mayor's coach passed the Bank on the 9th of November 1887.'

LEFT: William Logsdail's
*The Ninth of November,
1888*, 1890.

·ROBERTS' *ST PAUL'S FROM BLACKFRIARS WITH THE LORD MAYOR'S PROCESSION, 1862*·

·ANDREW GRAHAM-DIXON·

DAVID ROBERTS' PAINTING OF 1862, *St Paul's from Blackfriars*, shows the Lord Mayor passing over Blackfriars Bridge beneath the dome of St Paul's Cathedral. The painter deliberately chose a low viewpoint, so that he could include elements of the waterborne procession as well as the coaches and crowds above. Festive barges festooned with bright flags glide along the surface of the Thames amidst a throng of more mundane working vessels, ragged sails ruffled by a light breeze.

Roberts was a topographical painter by trade, having spent much of his life travelling through Spain, Italy, Egypt and the Near East, creating picturesque images of exotic, faraway places which were much admired by the British public. The most prominent of Victorian art critics, John Ruskin, wrote that 'with unwearied industry both in Egypt and Spain he brought home records of which the value is now forgotten in the perfect detail of photography, and sensational realism of the effects of light.' Roberts was in fact less of a realist than Ruskin believed. Like many another topographical artist he had a habit of improving on the truth by blending details remembered from more than one scene into a single image. The Lord Mayor's Show takes place in November, but the sky in *St Paul's from Blackfriars* looks more like a summer sky, with a few wispy clouds floating in a haze of heat. Roberts had made his studies for the picture in the summer of 1860, which may partly explain the unseasonal sunshine bathing an ostensibly

winter scene. But it seems to have been his intention from the outset to create an idealized image of London, in which bright memories of the past were to outshine the dark and dull realities of the present.

BELOW: David Roberts' *St Paul's from Blackfriars with the Lord Mayor's Procession*, 1862.

'Yesterday I made a sketch from the Blackfriars Bridge,' Roberts wrote to a friend in August 1860,

> which was not very pleasant, for I had some very ragged customers round me. Still the more I see of my proposed work the more I am convinced I have fallen on a mine of wealth in good subjects. True, I have to get into all sorts of disagreeable places, such as coal-wharves, lime-wharves, etc, for, from the number of steamers plying on the river, it is impossible to sit in a boat with safety, and the work must be done now or never, as the proposed new embankment will completely change the appearance of the river and its picturesque adjuncts.

Roberts was near the end of his life – he would die of a stroke in 1864, just two years after completing the picture – and it is hard to escape the impression that, as he wandered the coal-wharves and lime-wharves of the industrialized eastern reaches of the Thames, he was watching not just the flow of a river but also the flow of time. Born into a desperately poor family in Stockbridge, a suburb of Edinburgh, Roberts had first moved to London as an aspiring young painter in 1822. His wife, a beautiful Scottish actress called Margaret McLachlan, turned out to be an alcoholic, leaving him to bring up their daughter Christine alone. By the early 1860s that was all water (and whisky) under the bridge, but Roberts was increasingly troubled by what his contemporary and supporter Ruskin called 'the dark storm cloud of the nineteenth century' – the trauma of the Industrial Revolution. Nowhere were its effects more visible than in London, which had become almost unrecognizable from the city he had moved to as a young man. Sailboats on the Thames had been replaced by steam tugs and ferries, and the atmosphere itself had been so altered by coal-fired pollution that the whole city was shrouded, much of the time, in a thick yellowish smog.

Roberts was an indirect beneficiary of London's shuddering transformation into the world's busiest industrial metropolis. His principal patron, and the first owner of the picture reproduced here, was Charles Lucas, a rich contractor whose company constructed the Metropolitan and District Lines of the London Underground, as well as the Albert Hall. But as that letter of 1860 suggests, Roberts remained unreconciled to the physical changes undergone by the city he loved, hence his remark about the work having to be done 'now or never', before the cityscape was subjected to another wrenching alteration. In truth Roberts was not only stopping the clock, but turning it back, creating a picture of London not as it was in 1862, when he completed his picture, but as it had been in 1822, when he first arrived there. Hence the absence of smog from his painting, the profusion of sailing boats and barges, the glaring lack of any steam vessels at all. A critic reviewing the painting for *Blackwood's Magazine* remarked that it looked more like a depiction of Venice than London, complaining that 'we fail to recognise, whether in figures or shipping, the traffic that is really peculiar to our river. In point of fact Mr Roberts has treated us to a foreign importation.'

The critic missed the point. Roberts was not being inaccurate, but deliberately nostalgic. Earlier in his career, working in Egypt, he had spent much time around archaeologists, and perhaps his picture was itself intended to serve an archaeological purpose – preserving, in paint, the memory of a London that had already, during his lifetime, been almost entirely buried. Not long after completing the painting Roberts imagined a future in which London, like ancient Rome, would have fallen into ruins. What would survive of it then? Nothing perhaps, except 'in some national gallery, far away maybe in Timbuctoo, a representation of what London once was.'

· CRUIKSHANK'S *THE LORD MAYOR'S SHOW IN LUDGATE HILL* ·

· TIM CLAYTON ·

GEORGE CRUIKSHANK MADE THIS LITTLE steel etching, *The Lord Mayor's Show in Ludgate Hill*, to illustrate the month of November in his *Comic Almanack* of 1836. It shows the Lord Mayor's gilded coach rattling along Ludgate Hill, followed by a man in armour on horseback and a barge. In the foreground the crowd lining the street is being forced back by 'Peelers' armed with truncheons (Robert Peel's Metropolitan Police Force was founded in 1829); scuffles are breaking out, and in the confusion children are busily picking pockets – gangs of pickpockets notoriously preyed along the route. More fortunate spectators throng the upper windows of the shops of 1–4 Ludgate Hill, which are accurately depicted: the Albion Insurance Company; George Rich, venison dealer and confectioner; and T & G Baker, linen drapers and silk mercers. Rich advertises prime venison and real turtle soup; West Indian turtles had become the favourite dish at City banquets.

Cruikshank was the leading comic artist of his time. In his own words, he was 'cradled in caricature', helping his father, the illustrator and caricaturist Isaac Cruikshank, from earliest youth. By the age of 20 he had won a reputation as the most talented caricaturist after James Gillray, who had by then lapsed into insanity. Cruikshank produced a series of hilarious prints of Napoleon before turning his attention to the Prince Regent and his womanizing, party-loving spendthrift ways, in alliance with reformers such as his

friend William Hone. During the 1820s Cruikshank turned to book illustration for graphic series such as *Life in London*, a project celebrating London nightlife into which Cruikshank threw himself wholeheartedly. Like his father, who died after winning a drinking bout, he was a riotous hedonist and this made him an unreliable collaborator. Hone complained that he could not make progress with his publications 'without my friend George Cruikshank will forswear late hours, blue ruin [gin], and dollies', and that telling him this only drew the reply 'Go to Hell'.

Nevertheless, his illustrations for *German Popular Stories*, the first English translation of fairy tales by the Brothers Grimm, won him a reputation as an illustrator, and after he married in 1827 he worked more steadily. Cruikshank designed illustrations for 19 *Comic Almanacks* for the years between 1835 and 1853. Each contained a brief comic introduction, an illustration and a sheet of letterpress text for each month, and some pages of advertisements. The author of the first three volumes was James Henry Vizetelly, who adopted the pseudonym Rigdum Funidos. When Vizetelly died in 1838 Cruikshank persuaded the publisher Charles Tilt to hire William Makepeace Thackeray to create the letterpress for 1839 and 1840. Cruikshank's

illustrations showed appropriate scenes from London life for the month, for specific holidays such as Boxing Day or Valentine's Day, or the amusing consequences of March winds or April showers.

The *Comic Almanack* began well, with a circulation approaching 20,000, and it provided Cruikshank's principal source of income. It parodied *Old Moore's Almanack*: Francis Moore, a court astrologer during the reign of Charles II, had founded this publication in 1697, and, although he died in 1715, his publication was still being issued in 2015. Almanacs traditionally combined calendars with all sorts of other useful facts. Originally they were dominated by astronomical phenomena, from the phases of the moon to dramatic events like eclipses and comets, and accompanied by astrological predictions, which remained very popular.

By the end of the 18th century, half a million almanacs were published each year, including helpful information such as the fares charged by hackney coaches and watermen, but the bestselling *Old Moore's* continued to peddle astrology, which the *Comic Almanack* mocked as nonsense.

By this time Cruikshank had a very considerable reputation as a satirist and as an artist of the urban landscape. In 1836 he was working with Charles Dickens on *Sketches by 'Boz'*: the pair were hired by Richard Bentley to edit and illustrate *Bentley's Miscellany*, for which Cruikshank produced celebrated images for Dickens' *Oliver Twist*. Indeed Dickens, who was just breaking through, was dubbed by the *Spectator* at the close of that year as 'the CRUIKSHANK of writers'.

· HANNAH SCALLY ·

'Never! Nor, in fact, ever *was* there — or ever *will there be* in any city, upon any river in the world, such unapproachable and splendacious pageantry.'

— *The Illustrated London News*, 15 November 1845

OF ALL THE SUBJECTS COVERED BY *The Illustrated London News*, the Lord Mayor's Show was a favourite from the start. This event was a perfect whirl of glamour and visual sensation: celebrities, crowds, noisy entertainment and a lavish banquet to top it off. *The Illustrated London News* specialized in covering such magnificent public occasions. The world's first illustrated newspaper, it launched in 1842 at the dawn of a media revolution. Its dramatic pictures made all the difference for readers used to dense inky newspapers crammed with text. Now, people could view illustrations of the latest events not long after they occurred. There had never been anything like it. The paper became a giant of Victorian journalism, quickly achieving a circulation of up to 300,000 per issue.

No accident then that the paper's famous masthead featured the Lord Mayor's river procession with St Paul's Cathedral dominating the skyline. From its first year of publication the paper covered the Show in enthusiastic detail. The front page promised an 'abundance of embellishments' to capture 'the festival of Lord Mayor's Day, partly to gratify our readers

generally, and those particularly who are shut out by distance from the scene'. Not to miss an opportunity for publicity, representatives of the paper even joined the Show that year, with a boat full of men wearing *Illustrated London News* sandwich boards sailing ahead of the river procession.

ABOVE: Samuel Begg's picture of the Lord Mayor's Banquet in 1904 is full of human intimacy and photographic realism, bringing readers to the heart of the celebration.

Coverage in that first year stretched across four pages, with two given over to an enormous, snaking illustration of the land procession. This and other scenes were sketchy in style, intricate and exploding with life. They were the work of John Gilbert, a versatile artist who made his name in pictorial journalism at the paper. Gilbert produced an estimated 30,000 illustrations over his long career, and public spectacle was his speciality. But he didn't work alone. Even illustrations by a single artist depended on a skilled team of engravers and printers, working together and often signing work alongside the artist. Like the Show itself, newspapers were fundamentally collaborative.

For many, shared memory and shared experience were the essence of Lord Mayor's Day. The paper depicted the people of London: crowds lining the street, small groups waiting for the Show, *vox populi* and vignettes. The heritage of the City was just as important, so coverage was peppered with anecdotes and illustrations of Shows from centuries past.

Attention nevertheless waxed and waned. Some years the Show appeared only in complaints about its cost and predictability. In other years, the paper went all out in rapturous coverage. With photography dominating the paper by the 1920s, *The Illustrated London News* — by then an institution in its own right — brought new, living visions of the Show to its readers. Well into the 20th century, the paper revisited the Show and its people with warm familiarity, even as new media began to overtake the weekly newspaper.

For a century before the rise of television, *The Illustrated London News* was the closest thing to a live broadcast of the Lord Mayor's Show. Today it contributes to the record of the Show's glorious past. It is fitting then that *The Illustrated London News* was commissioned in the 1970s to produce the Show's programme for several years, and, in the year when the Show celebrates its 800th anniversary, *The Illustrated London News* — now a creative content agency — has been reappointed from 2015 to publish the programme anew.

· THE SHOW IN HITCHCOCK'S *SABOTAGE* ·

· PIERRE LETHIER ·

AUTUMN 1935, AND THE TRIUMPH OF *The 39 Steps* was still fresh in the collective memory when its prodigious young director, Alfred Hitchcock, decided to dabble once again in the murky world of British politics. This time the setting was to be the pomp and poverty of London. *Sabotage*, Hitchcock's fourth tale of clandestine agents during the interwar years, is an ambitious and original screen adaptation, at once a liberal updating and faithful distillation of the essence of Joseph Conrad's novel *The Secret Agent* (1907), which by the 1930s was already well established as a literary classic.

Hitchcock had barely sketched out his screenplay when he let the cameramen and sound engineers of his second unit loose on the streets of the metropolis. It was the second Saturday in November, and Hitchcock wanted to capture the chaotic atmosphere of the heaving crowd which had come to watch the grand procession of the Lord Mayor's Show. His aim was to amass as many visual markers of the Show as possible as it proceeded past the Royal Courts of Justice, and to record a plethora of sounds – in particular the marches, anthems and fanfares blasted out by the heralds at the head of the Lord Mayor's State Coach.

The challenge Hitchcock set himself in *Sabotage* was to contrast the jubilation of the well-heeled denizens of London's western districts (where he himself now resided) and the fortitude and good cheer of the

BELOW LEFT: Sylvia Sidney, Alfred Hitchcock and John Loder between takes.

BELOW: A man selling penny panoramas of the Show displays his wares to Stevie.

ABOVE: The procession passing the film set of the Royal Courts of Justice during the making of the film.

Alpine retreat. Taking the interior world of the characters as his focus, Hitchcock created a potent cocktail of suspense, deception and fear. The film's plot is constructed around the seductive and ill-starred wife of the saboteur, Winnie Verloc, played by the young American star of film noir Sylvia Sidney, straight from her performance in Fritz Lang's *Fury*. While *Sabotage* is in every sense an authentic Hitchcock adventure story, its peculiar, vertiginous exploration of grief makes it an unusual work within the director's British filmmaking period. The grief in question is not only that of the lead character Winnie, an innocent who soon turns to vengeance, but also that of the entire nation, already bruised by the experience of the royal abdication and now to be cruelly wounded by a terrorist attack. The terrorists deliberately choose to target a venerable, centuries-old ceremony in a symbolic assault on the stability of institutions and grand tradition. Their aim on that famous November morning is no less than to reduce Piccadilly Circus to ashes.

The sinister saboteur Verloc (played by Oscar Homolka), the lazy and venal owner of a suburban movie theatre, and his even more sinister accomplice, a bird shop owner known only as The Professor (William Dewhurst), agree to detonate a time bomb in Piccadilly Circus underground station. However, when he discovers that Scotland Yard are on his tail, Verloc backs out of doing the deed himself, instead tricking his brother-in-law Stevie (Desmond Tester), a dim-witted adolescent, into carrying out the crime by getting him to deliver a package of film reels in which he has hidden the explosive. Hitchcock slows Stevie down and racks up the tension, making him stop and watch the procession for what seems like an age. The bomb eventually does explode, but on the bus between the Strand and Piccadilly...

inhabitants of the East End (where he originally hailed from), with the morbid, nihilistic folly and despair of the villainous agents. These revolutionaries of the 1930s Depression – the distant successors of Conrad's saboteurs – are apparently devoid of any ideological commitment, little more than fly-by-night mercenaries hired by a shadowy totalitarian foreign power.

The fragments of newsreel footage captured on that sunny November in 1935 were incorporated nearly a year later into the film's brief but highly significant parade sequence. Hitchcock had to reconstruct the Royal Courts of Justice on a gigantic studio set, but his audience – at the first screening, at any rate – will not have noticed this artifice at the point in the film when the newly appointed Lord Mayor takes the oath of allegiance required by his ancient and prestigious office, a joyful crowd surging after his coach.

In January 1936 Hitchcock and his inseparable screenwriter Charles Bennett put together this contemporary tragedy in the comfort of the director's

· JAMES BOND AND THE LORD MAYOR'S SHOW ·

· PIERRE LETHIER ·

THERE CAN BE LITTLE DOUBT THAT BY the winter of 1957 both Ian Fleming and his young but enduring creation, James Bond, were in serious need of some rest and recuperation – a breather of sorts, but also a return to their creative source, to the sun-drenched haven of the West Indies. The author was in need of respite from an exhausting period of research and writing, and from an overwhelming success he had hoped for but never realistically expected; his protagonist, meanwhile, needed time to recover from a terrible wound and a particularly violent neurotoxin which, to the distress of thousands of readers, had left him close to death in a suite at the Paris Ritz. Bond may have been intrepid, sombre and occasionally cruel, but his charm had won over legions of new admirers.

In his masterwork *From Russia with Love* Fleming had not only breathed life into the old format of the spy story but also offered a fascinating new take on the burgeoning Cold War. In this, 007's fifth epic outing, the omnipresent narrator who had thrown himself headlong into a thrilling adventure on the Orient Express was immediately and justifiably lauded on both sides of the Atlantic. The new mania for Fleming's hero was showing no signs of fading when the sixth novel, *Dr No*, set in the relaxed colonial environment of Jamaica, was published in April 1958 and founded the James Bond myth in earnest.

The novel has a superlative, dreamlike quality, freely given to excess and flamboyance. *Dr No*

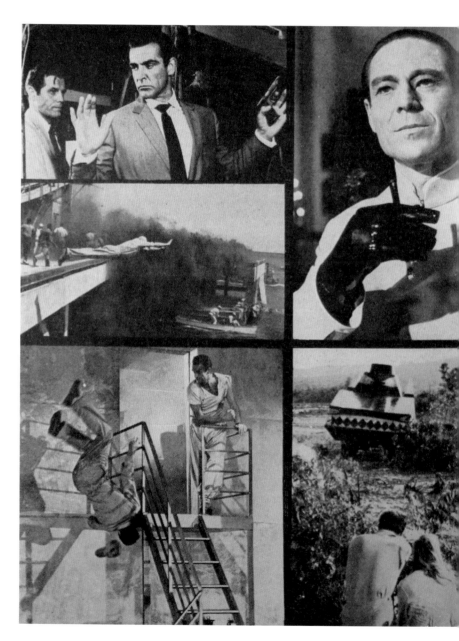

THE FIRST JAMES BOND FILM!

HARRY SALTZMAN and ALBERT R. BROCCOLI PRESENT

IAN FLEMING'S

Dr NO

TECHNICOLOR

SEAN CONNERY

URSULA ANDRESS · JOSEPH WISEMAN · JACK LORD · ANTHONY DAWSON · MARSHALL KITZMILLER · GAYSON · ALSO STARRING BERNARD LEE

Screenplay by RICHARD MAIBAUM · JOHANNA HARWOOD · BERKELY MATHER · Directed by TERENCE YOUNG · Produced by HARRY SALTZMAN and ALBERT R. BROCCOLI · EON PRODUCTIONS

ABOVE: The original 1962 movie poster, designed by Mitchell Hooks.

OPPOSITE: Movie stills from the inside front cover of the comic book adaptation of *Dr No*, Showcase #43, published by DC Comics in 1963. The dragon buggy is bottom right.

established the recipe for the Bond saga, and as such it is unsurprising that it was the first of Fleming's 14 Bond novels to be adapted for the silver screen. 'M', the austere and calculating head of intelligence – a figure more reminiscent of Macmillan than Eden in an age troubled by the disastrous Suez affair – lifts Bond from months of boredom in hospital and sends him to Kingston to complete his convalescence. The plan is to give him a simple routine mission – to lay his hands on local branch chief John Strangways, who is roundly suspected of having deserted the secret service and slipped away quietly with his seductive assistant Mary Trueblood. The illusion of an amorous escapade only serves to aggravate the bigotry and somnolence of the crusty old administration. Bond embarks on a labyrinthine quest which takes him to the dark recesses of a virtually forgotten island between Jamaica and Cuba, Crab Key, and pits him in a range of deadly encounters – from brushes with venomous spiders to single combat against a giant squid – whose improbability incensed the poisoned pens of the critics, an inevitable consequence of Fleming's success the previous year. Bond eventually escapes from the curious hell into which his boss has pitched him in a black-and-gold-painted dragon buggy stolen from his adversary.

And then comes the image which, at a stroke, sets this fable in its wider political context. In the words of Fleming's protagonist, his getaway vehicle is 'a dragon that looked like a float waiting for the Lord Mayor's Show'. The jubilant metaphor is a triumph, a long-awaited injection of redeeming humour allied to a fairy-tale visual composition of pink flamingos, rare spoonbills and, most conspicuously, Honeychile Rider, a latter-day Venus rising naked from the waves, more beautiful, more perfect (in Bond parlance) than Sandro Botticelli's. Bond makes his escape on the ersatz mayoral float having plucked this divine, wild Venus orchid from a heap of manure – literally, a mountain of guano or cormorant excrement. This foul-smelling but profitable natural fertilizer acts as a cover for the true activities of Dr Julius No, the new Fu Manchu of the spy genre, who in a luxury underground city is acting on behalf of Soviet interests in the Caribbean, directing a facility which blocks radioelectric transmissions at American missile testing sites on the nearby Turks Islands – for good measure he also runs a laboratory where he experiments on live human subjects. Strangways, along with several members of a charitable society established to protect the native roseate spoonbills, has unwisely strayed to the pestilential shores of Crab Key and paid with his life. In a matter of a few lines Ian Fleming, who had foreseen the change in both colonial rule and the balance of power in the Caribbean, buries Bond's enemy under several tons of excrement. Meanwhile, Bond, recuperated and victorious, rallies Her Majesty's young military commanders to his cause – the Empire is still effective and Britain must be defended across her dominions. Bond's dragon buggy, in its association with one of Britain's great enduring traditions, is an unorthodox, arresting and potent vehicle for that message.

·*HUMBERT, MR FIRKIN AND THE LORD MAYOR OF LONDON* ·

· JOHN BURNINGHAM ·

I have written and illustrated over 60 books; some for adults, most for children. One of my favourite stories, published in 1965, is *Humbert, Mr Firkin and the Lord Mayor of London*. The story is this: Mr Firkin was a scrap-iron dealer and Humbert, his horse, would pull the cart that collected the scrap metal. Humbert used to see the horses that pulled the Lord Mayor's coach when Mr Firkin had lunch near the brewery where they were stabled. They were terrible snobs and thought they had a much better existence than Humbert! Humbert finally had his chance when, on the day of the Lord Mayor's Show, one of the wheels on the coach broke and the Lord Mayor was unable to proceed any further. A hush fell over the crowd. Officials rushed to the scene and suggested taking the Lord Mayor the rest of the way

BELOW: Humbert and Mr Firkin travelling through the streets of London.

ABOVE: The front cover of the first edition, with the Lord Mayor of London perched on an old gas cooker.

RIGHT: Humbert asleep in his stable with the cup presented to him by the Lord Mayor on the shelf.

by car. 'Motor cars?' he bellowed. 'Unheard of. Monstrous. On an occasion like this the Lord Mayor does not ride in a motorcar. Get me another coach or something.' Humbert, observing all this, pushed himself forward, even though the policemen and Mr Firkin tried to hold him back. To the dismay of the other horses, the Lord Mayor asked whether Humbert would be kind enough to help him finish his journey. And so the Lord Mayor is safely delivered to Mansion House – atop an old gas cooker.

To thank Humbert and Mr Firkin, they were invited to the Lord Mayor's Banquet, where they were guests of honour at the top table and the Lord Mayor presented Humbert with a special cup in memory of the occasion.

· ADRIAN STEEL ·

WALKING THROUGH THE STREETS OF the City of London, it is hard to miss the legacy of the postal service, and not just because of the iconic street furniture of red pillar boxes and phone kiosks. The Post Office has had a home in the City since shortly after King Charles I opened his Royal Mails to the public in 1635. A General Letter Office sat near Princes Street between 1653 and 1666, and a blue plaque now marks its role in striking the world's first postmarks. After the Restoration, the General Post Office (GPO) opened its headquarters on the south side of Lombard Street in the heart of the City. Before that, coffeehouses were often used for the sending and receiving of mail. Among the most famous of these was Lloyd's Coffee House; also situated on Lombard Street and today commemorated with a blue plaque, it played a pivotal role in the development of the City's now global insurance market.

Elsewhere in the City the legacies of the postal service can be seen in abundance. Postman's Park, which borders the site of a later GPO headquarters on St Martin's le Grand, is so named because it was frequented by postal workers, while on King Edward Street, a statue of Rowland Hill, whose postal reforms changed the face of global communication with the introduction of the Penny Black, stands as a permanent reminder of the Victorian ingenuity embodied by the Post Office. The GPO even took up residence under the City's streets: from 1927, beneath

the feet of thousands of workers, the subterranean Mail Rail moved mail between east and west London on the world's first driverless, automatic trains. For over 300 years, the City was at the forefront of the national, and international, communications revolution.

It is fitting, therefore, that the Post Office, Royal Mail and The Postal Museum (formerly the British Postal Museum & Archive) have been involved in the Lord Mayor's Show on many occasions. In 1970 a

ABOVE & RIGHT: The 1989 Lord Mayor's Show stamp issue illustrated by Paul Cox.

ABOVE: The 1982 Royal Mail float.

But the Post Office's association with the Lord Mayor's Show in modern times is perhaps best remembered with the stamp issue of October 1989. Released to mark the 800th anniversary of the office of the Lord Mayor of London, the Lord Mayor's Show commemorative stamp issue stemmed from a direct approach by Lord Mayor Sir Greville Spratt. With the schedule for stamp issues made years in advance, and a plan already in place for a 'regalia' stamp issue at the same time, the Royal Mail decided that the Lord Mayor's suggestion reflected such an important moment in national history that the regalia issue should be replaced with a set of five stamps collectively known as the Lord Mayor's Show issue.

replica 1910 post van and an 18th-century mail coach were featured, and in 2010 the British Postal Museum & Archive brought a piece of living history to the parade: GPO2, a 1936 mobile Post Office, once fully equipped with everything from phone kiosks to telegram desks, which had been in storage for many years. It was greeted with cheers from thousands of supporters along the route – a very British sight to behold.

Following submissions from various designers, Paul Cox, a freelance illustrator, was chosen for his colourful hand-drawn depictions of various elements of the Lord Mayor's Show that, when placed side by side, formed a horizontal panorama of the procession. The designs captured the Royal Mail coach, an escort of Blues and Royals, the Lord Mayor waving to the crowds from his coach, the Lord Mayor's State Coach passing St Paul's, and a Blues and Royals drum horse.

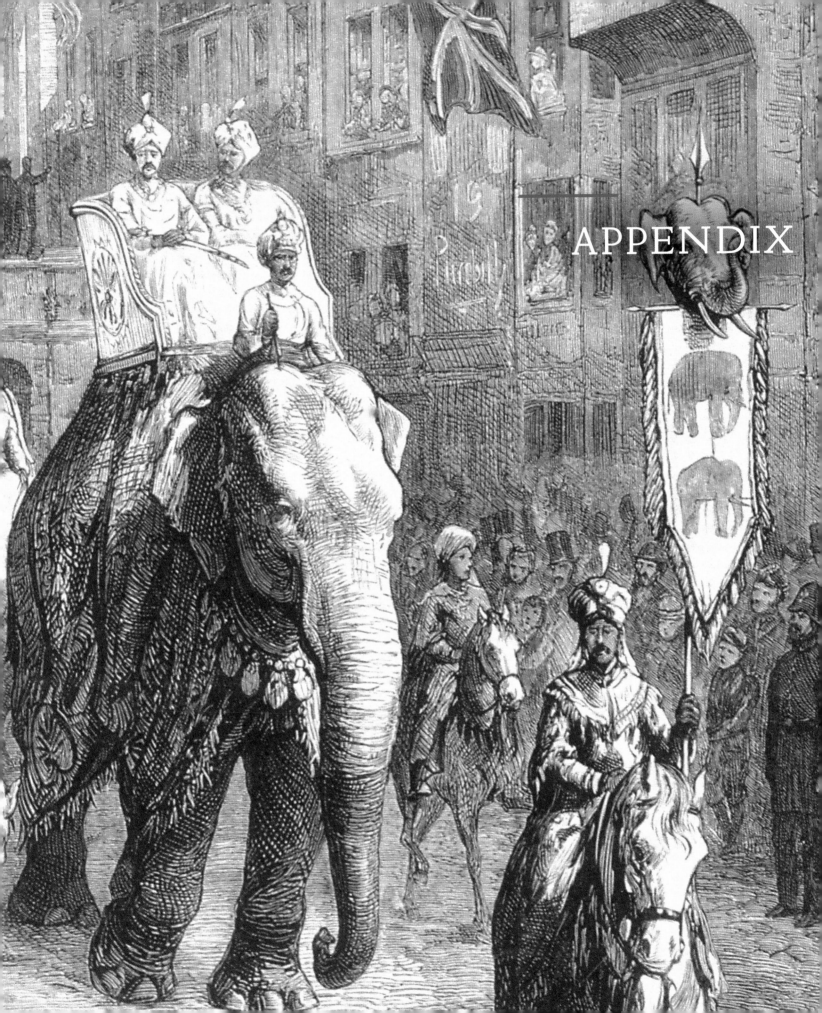

APPENDIX

· SOURCES AND FURTHER READING ·

CEREMONY & TRADITION

Eric Hobsbawm and Terence Ranger (eds), *The Invention of Tradition* (Cambridge: Cambridge University Press, 1983).

The Ceremonial Handbook of the Corporation of London.

Robert Withington, *English Pageantry: An Historical Outline* (New York: Benjamin Blom, 1963).

ARCHITECTURAL SETTING

Kenneth Allinson, *Architects and Architecture of London* (London: Routledge, 2008), p.89.

Caroline M. Barron, *The Medieval Guildhall of London* (London: Corporation of London, 1974), p.25.

Hazel Forsyth, *London's Lost Jewels: The Cheapside Hoard* (London: Museum of London and Philip Wilson Publishers, 2013), pp.20–1.

Tracey Hill, *Pageantry and Power: A Cultural History of the Early Modern Lord Mayor's Show 1585–1639* (Manchester: Manchester University Press, 2013).

Lane's Masonic Records.

James Ralph, *A Critical Review of the Public Buildings, Statues and Ornaments in and about London and Westminster*, 1783 edition, pp.36–7; quoted in Sally Jeffery, *The Mansion House* (Chichester: Phillimore, for the Corporation of London, 1993), pp.20–1.

John Stow, *A Survey of London*, 1603 edition, reprinted 1908 and edited by Charles L. Kingsford, vol. i, p.1, p.119.

Ben Weinreb and Christopher Hibbert (eds), *The London Encyclopaedia* (London: Macmillan, 1988), p.513.

Vertue Notebooks, Walpole Society, vol. 22, p.122.

THE LORD MAYOR'S BANQUET

John Ashton (text) and Francis Compton Price (drawings), *The Lord Mayor's Show in the Olden Times. Compiled from Various Authentic Drawings and Ancient MSS. Showing with Perfect Accuracy the 'Pageants' and Allegorical Structures Which Commonly Accompanied the Lord Mayor in His 'Ride' from Guildhall to Westminster, in the 15th and 16th Centuries, with Views of the Principal City Buildings, Including Guildhall, Royal Exchange, Bow Church, Cheape Cross, and London Bridge* (London: Charles Letts & Co., 1883).

Anon., attributed to Sir Charles Flower and George Cruikshank (frontispiece illustration), *The Jubilee, and Civic Debates on the Jubilee Dinner, Travestis. Dedicated to All Lovers of the True Sublime*, 2nd edition (London: T. Tegg, 1809).

Peregrine Pettitoe (pseud), *Grief a-La-Mode, a City Dream, on the Death of Lord Mayor's Day (in the Disappointment of a Dinner). A Visionary Lesson for Fashion and Folly. Dedicated to the Masters and Wardens of the Several Companies; and Offered as a Morsel of Amusement in the Sad Hour of Mourning. By Their Devoted Servant, a City Cook* (London: sold by Kemmish et al., 1786).

Edward Ward, *O Raree-Show, O Pretty-Show: Or, the City Feast* (London, 1698).

THE LORD MAYOR'S SEAL

Jonathan Alexander and Paul Binski (eds), *Age of Chivalry: Art in Plantagenet England 1200–1400* (London: Royal Academy of Arts and Weidenfeld and Nicolson, 1987), pp.273–4.

Caroline M. Barron, 'The Political Culture of Medieval London' in Linda Clark and Christine Carpenter (eds), *The Fifteenth Century Volume IV: The Political Culture of Late Medieval Britain* (Woodbridge: Boydell Press, 2004), pp.110–133.

COACHBUILDING IN LONDON

Rudolf Wackernagel, 'Carlton House Mews: The State Coach of the Prince of Wales and of the later King of Hanover. A Study in the Late-Eighteenth-Century 'Mystery' of Coach Building', *Furniture History*, vol. 31, 1995, pp.47–115.

COSTUME & REGALIA

Caroline M. Barron, 'Chivalry, Pageantry and Merchant Culture in Medieval London', in Peter Coss and Maurice Keen (eds), *Heraldry, Pageantry and Social Display in Medieval England* (Woodbridge: Boydell Press, 2002), pp.219–41.

D. Fletcher, 'The Lancastrian Collar of Esses: Its Origins and Transformations Down the Centuries', in James L. Gillespie (ed.), *The Age of Richard II* (Stroud: Sutton Publishing, 1997), pp.191–204.

A. D. Mansfield, *Ceremonial Costume: Court, Civil and Civic Costume from 1660 to the Present Day* (London: A & C Black, 1980).

WILLIAM WALWORTH & THE PEASANTS' REVOLT

R. B. Dobson (ed.), *The Peasants' Revolt of 1381*, 2nd edition (London: Macmillan, 1983). *[A collection of translated documentary sources for the Revolt.]*

Alastair Dunn, *The Great Rising of 1381* (Stroud: Tempus, 2002).

Pamela Nightingale, 'Sir William Walworth (d.1386?), merchant and mayor of London' in *Oxford Dictionary of National Biography* (Oxford: Oxford University Press, 2004).

PREVIOUS SPREAD: In 1876 13 elephants took part in the Show. In this illustration from *The Graphic* they are seen passing under Temple Bar.

RICHARD 'DICK' WHITTINGTON

Caroline M. Barron, 'Richard Whittington: the Man behind the Myth' in A. E. J. Hollaender and William Kellaway (eds), *Studies in London History Presented to Philip Edmund Jones* (London: Hodder and Stoughton, 1969), pp.197–248.

Carole Rawcliffe, 'Richard Whittington (d.1423)' in J. S. Roskell, Linda Clark and Carole Rawcliffe (eds), *The House of Commons 1386–1421*, 4 vols (Stroud: Alan Sutton, for the History of Parliament Trust, 1992), vol. IV, pp.846–49.

Anne F. Sutton, 'Richard (Dick) Whittington (c.1350–1423) merchant and mayor of London' in *Oxford Dictionary of National Biography* (Oxford: Oxford University Press, 2002).

EARLY MODERN PERIOD: PRIMARY SOURCES

Calendar of State Papers Venetian 1617–1619, vol. XV (London: 1909).

Thomas Dekker, *Londons tempe, or, The feild [sic] of happines* (London: Nicholas Okes, 1629).

Henry Machyn, ed. John Gough Nichols, *The Diary of Henry Machyn, Citizen and Merchant Taylor of London, from AD 1550 to AD 1563* (London: J. B. Nichols and Son, 1848).

Thomas Middleton, *The triumphs of health and prosperity* (London: Nicholas Okes, 1626).

Anthony Munday, ed. J. G. Nichols, *Chrysanaleia, the Golden Fishing* (London: printed for the Worshipful Company of Fishmongers, 1844).

Anthony Munday, *Chrysanaleia: the golden fishing; or, Honour of fishmongers* (London: George Purslowe, 1616).

Thomas Nelson, *The deuice of the pageant: set forth by the worshipfull companie of the fishmongers, for the right honorable Iohn Allot* (London, 1590; STC 18423).

George Peele, *The deuice of the pageant borne before Woolstone Dixi Lord Maior of the citie of London* (London: Edward Allde, 1585; STC 19533).

George Peele, *Descensus astraeae the device of a l'ageant [sic], borne before M. William Web* (London: printed for William Wright, 1591; STC 19532).

Lupold von Wedel, 'Journey through England and Scotland made by Lupold von Wedel in the years 1584 and 1585', trans. Gottfried von Bülow, *Transactions of the Royal Historical Society*, 9 (1895), pp.223–70.

EARLY MODERN PERIOD: SECONDARY SOURCES

David M. Bergeron, *English Civic Pageantry 1558–1642*, revised edition (Tucson: University of Arizona, 2003).

Tracey Hill, *Anthony Munday and Civic Culture* (Manchester: Manchester University Press, 2004).

Tracey Hill, *Pageantry and Power: A Cultural History of the Early Modern Lord Mayor's Show* (Manchester: Manchester University Press, 2010).

Emma Kennedy, 'Not Barren of Invention': Texts, Context and Intertexts of the London Lord Mayor's Shows, 1614–1619 (PhD thesis, University of York, 2014).

Anne Lancashire, *London Civic Theatre* (Cambridge: Cambridge University Press, 2002).

Lawrence Manley, *Literature and Culture in Early Modern London* (Cambridge: Cambridge University Press, 1995).

Kenneth Nicholls Palmer, *Ceremonial Barges on the River Thames* (London: Unicorn Press, 1997).

CARICATURE & GRAPHIC SATIRE

Edward Du Cann, *The Duke of Wellington and his Political Career After Waterloo – The Caricaturists' View* (Woodbridge: Antique Collectors' Club, 2000).

Dorothy George, *Hogarth to Cruikshank: Social Change in Graphic Satire*, revised edition (London: Viking, 1987).

Elizabeth Longford, *Wellington: Pillar of State* (London: Weidenfeld and Nicolson, 1972).

Brian Maidment, *Comedy, Caricature and the Social Order 1820–1850* (Manchester: Manchester University Press, 2013).

THE WAR YEARS

City Press, 6 & 13 November 1915, 10 November 1939, 15 November 1940, 14 November 1941, 13 November 1942, 12 November 1943, 10 November 1944, 9 November 1945.

Daily Mirror, 10 November 1915.

The Manchester Guardian, 7 November 1915.

The Times, 6, 8, 9 & 10 November 1915, 9 November 1939, 11 November 1941, 10 November 1942, 10 November 1943, 10 November 1945, 11 November 1946, 11 November 1947, 10 November 1948, 10 November 1949.

Official Programme for Lord Mayor's Day, 1941, etc, London Metropolitan Archives COL/RMD/05/01/005/001.

Lord Mayor's Day, 1946, file in London Metropolitan Archives, COL/RMD/05/01/005/004.

FILM FOOTAGE

British Pathé: www.britishpathe.com

NOTE

The London Metropolitan Archives holds a wealth of resources relating to the Lord Mayor's Show.

CAROLINE BARRON is Emeritus Professor of the History of London at Royal Holloway, University of London. Her interests include the study of medieval women, the reign of Richard II, the religious life of medieval lay people and all aspects of life in medieval London. Her book *London in the Later Middle Ages: Government and People 1200–1500* was published by Oxford University Press in 2004. She is currently working on the reading habits of medieval Londoners and, in particular, their experiments (largely unsuccessful) in more radical forms of government.

BEATRICE BEHLEN has been studying and working in the fields of fashion, dress history, design and art – mostly in museums and art colleges, including Historic Royal Palaces and, at present, the Museum of London – ever since discovering the dress history section of her parents' encyclopedia. She is particularly curious about people, their biography and how it relates to the things they have left behind.

JEREMY BLACK is Professor of History at the University of Exeter. Graduating from Cambridge with a starred first, he did postgraduate work at Oxford, and then taught at Durham before moving to Exeter. He has lectured extensively in Australia, Canada, Denmark, France, Germany, Italy, New Zealand and the US, where he has held visiting chairs at West Point, Texas Christian University and Stillman College. His books include *The British Seaborne Empire* (2004), *Contesting History* (2014) and *Rethinking World War Two* (2015).

MELVYN BRAGG was born in Wigton, Cumbria, and educated there and at Wadham College, Oxford. His broadcasting career began at the BBC in 1961 and soon afterwards he published his first novel. He worked on *Monitor* with Huw Wheldon in the mid-1960s, and collaborated with Ken Russell,

writing a film about Tchaikovsky, *The Music Lovers* (1970). He also wrote *Isadora*, directed by Karel Reisz, *Play Dirty* starring Michael Caine, and worked with David Lean. In 1977 Melvyn started LWT's *The South Bank Show*, making about 750 editions as well as other documentaries. In the meantime he has expanded his range, presenting arts and science programmes and marshalling discussion shows on BBC Radio (on *In Our Time*), and writing non-fiction books including *The Adventure of English*, *The King James Bible* and *On Giants' Shoulders*. Over the past 50 years he has continued to write novels. He is an Honorary Fellow of the Royal Society and of The British Academy, and was given a Peerage in 1998.

JOHN BURNINGHAM is a much-loved children's author and illustrator whose books include *Borka: The Adventures of a Goose With No Feathers* (1963), *Mr Gumpy's Outing* (1970), *Would You Rather…* (1978), *Avocado Baby* (1982) and *The Way to the Zoo* (2014). He has won the Kate Greenaway Medal twice and twice been a finalist for the prestigious Hans Christian Andersen Award.

TIM CLAYTON is an author and historian working on military history and on visual print culture during the long 18th century. He was co-curator of the exhibition 'Bonaparte and the British: Prints and Propaganda in the Age of Napoleon' at the British Museum in 2015, and his most recent book, *Waterloo: Four Days that Changed Europe's Destiny* (2014), was highly acclaimed.

TIM CONNELL is an Emeritus Professor of City University and a Life Fellow of Gresham College. He is a Freeman of the City of London and a Liveryman of the Worshipful Company of Stationers and Newspaper Makers, where he sits on the Court. He writes and speaks regularly on a range of topics relating to London.

DAN CRUICKSHANK is the author of several books on London, including *London: The Art of Georgian Building* (1975) and *The Secret History of Georgian London* (2009). He is a broadcaster making culture and travel programmes for the BBC, has served on the executive committee of The Georgian Group, on the Architectural Panel of the National Trust, was a Visiting Professor at the University of Sheffield, is an Honorary Fellow of the Royal Institute of British Architects and a Freeman of the City of London.

JOHN DAVIS has been a Fellow in History at The Queen's College, Oxford, since 1989, specializing in the history of post-war London. He is currently working on restaurants and 'eating out' in the capital in the 1960s and 1970s.

TOM FOAKES is Curator of the Museum of the Order of St John, Clerkenwell. In this role he has overseen the creation of new museum galleries, which reopened to the public in 2010 following a £4.1m redevelopment project. He is a Freeman of the City, a Liveryman of the Draper's Company, and a Freeman of the Company of Art Scholars.

JOHN FRANKLIN is Head Master of Christ's Hospital, one of Britain's foremost boarding schools in the independent sector, its mission virtually unchanged since its foundation. Previously Headmaster of Ardingly and Deputy Headmaster of St Peter's College, Adelaide, he has also held posts at Marlborough and Sedbergh.

MARTIN GAYFORD has written books about Van Gogh, Constable and Michelangelo and published a volume of conversations with David Hockney. Lucian Freud painted and etched his portrait, an experience he described in *Man with a Blue Scarf* (2010). He is art critic of *The Spectator*.

THE GENTLE AUTHOR writes about the culture of the East End and the City daily at www.spitalfieldslife.com, and is the author of a number of bestselling books including *Spitalfields Life* (2012) and *The Gentle Author's London Album* (2013).

DAVID GIBBS taught at Sherborne School, Charterhouse and Haileybury before serving as Headmaster at Chigwell School (1996–2007). Subsequently he was Education Officer at the Skinners' Company, involved especially in the creation of three transformational academies. He is the author of several books on educational history.

ANDREW GRAHAM-DIXON is one of the UK's leading art critics, having presented numerous landmark series for the BBC including the acclaimed *A History of British Art, Renaissance* and the popular *Italy Unpacked* with chef Giorgio Locatelli. For over 20 years he wrote a weekly column for *The Independent* and latterly *The Sunday Telegraph*. He has published several books, the most recent being *Caravaggio: A Life Sacred and Profane*.

MARIA HAYWARD is Professor of History at the University of Southampton. She works on textiles and clothing at the Tudor and Stuart courts. Her books include *Dress at the Court of King Henry VIII* (2007) and *Rich Apparel: Clothing and the Law in Henry VIII's England* (2009).

TRACEY HILL is Head of English at Bath Spa University. She specializes in the literature and cultural history of early modern London and is the author of two books, both published by Manchester University Press: *Anthony Munday and Civic Culture* (2004) and *Pageantry and Power: A Cultural History of the Early Modern Lord Mayor's Show, 1585–1639* (2010), which won the David Bevington Award in 2011.

WILLIAM HUNT, Windsor Herald, a Past Master of the Worshipful Company of Makers of Playing Cards, has designed the Arms of the majority of the Sheriffs in the past 20 years. A veteran of 26 Shows, marching either with The Honourable Artillery Company or as a Marshal, he is a Lieutenant of the City, a past Member of the Court of Common Council and serves on the Executive Committee of the City Association of the Reserve Forces' and Cadets' Association (RFCA).

PIERRE LETHIER is a Fellow of the Buckingham University Centre for Security and Intelligence Studies. Following a career as a senior intelligence officer with the French foreign branch, he moved into Film Studies. Over the last ten years he has lectured extensively and published numerous essays on the spy film and war film genres in both the UK and US, including regular contributions for the think tank RUSI (Royal United Services Institute), for the department of War Studies at King's College London, for the universities of Brunel and Warwick, and for the British Film Institute.

JANE LEVI is a writer specializing in food and utopianism and a visiting research fellow at King's College London. She combines research and teaching with occasional consultancy in the City of London, where she worked on regulatory matters for many years before completing her PhD in cultural history.

BRIAN MAIDMENT is Professor of the History of Print at Liverpool John Moores University. He has written widely on the 19th century, especially on mass-circulation magazines and visual culture. His most recent book is *Comedy, Caricature and the Social Order 1820–1850* (2013).

JAMES NORTH is the Swordbearer to the Lord Mayor, the 57th incumbent of the post since it was first established in 1417. He is the Senior Esquire to the Lord Mayor, responsible for delivering the Lord Mayor's ceremonial events in the City. He joined Mansion House in 2008, working as a Programme Manager and undertaking the planning and organization of a share of the Mayoralty's domestic programme and overseas business visits.

DOMINIC REID has been Pageantmaster of the Lord Mayor's Show longer than anyone in history. Educated at Oundle, Cambridge University and UCL, he is responsible for every aspect of the Show. He is a Governor of the Museum of London, Honorary Colonel of the City of London & NE Sector Army Cadet Force, a Lieutenant of the City of London, and a Liveryman of the Grocers' Company. He was appointed OBE for services to the City of London in 2003.

HANNAH SCALLY is a historian of 19th-century cultural history. Originally from Ireland, she completed a PhD at the University of Cambridge on 19th-century business culture. She is Senior Historian at Illustrated London News Ltd.

ADRIAN STEEL is Director of The Postal Museum, formerly the British Postal Museum & Archive. Since 2006 he has led an ambitious project to create a new, national visitor attraction, bringing five centuries of Britain's social and communications history into the public domain and opening up the Post Office's own underground railway – the Mail Rail – to visitors for the first time. He holds a PhD in History and an MA in Archives and Records Management.

CATHERINE STIRK is a Producer in BBC Events, part of BBC Entertainment and Events Production. She has worked on some of the biggest outside broadcasts in recent years including World War One Remembered, The Funeral of Baroness Thatcher and The Royal Wedding. More recently she has produced the Lord Mayor's Show and The Queen's Christmas Broadcast.

NICHOLAS VINCENT is Professor of Medieval History at the University of East Anglia and a leading expert on Magna Carta and its background. His books include *Magna Carta: The Foundation of Freedom 1215–2015* (2015) and *Magna Carta: A Very Short Introduction* (2012).

ANDREW WALLIS is Curator of The Guards Museum near Buckingham Palace. He is Captain of the Lord Mayor's ceremonial bodyguard, The Company of Pikemen & Musketeers, having served in the bodyguard for 20 years and in The Honourable Artillery Company for 42 years. He was formerly a director of Deutsche Bank.

ALEX WERNER is Head of History Collections at the Museum of London, where he oversees the management and curatorial development of the museum's post-1700 collection. He has lectured and written widely on London's historic port and river. His publications include *Dockland Life* (2000), *London's Changing Riverscape* (2009), *Dickens's Victorian London* (2011) and *Sherlock Holmes* (2014).

· LIST OF SUBSCRIBERS ·

Petty Officer A. J. C. Adams
Mary Adlard
The Allington Family
Peter Alvey
Barbara Anderson
J. Douglas Anderson
Mark Andrew
N. C. Andrew
The Andrews Family
George R. A. Andrews
Rick and Vicki Andrews
Nick and Claire Anstee
The Society of Apothecaries
Ingrid Appleby-Hopwood
Mark Arbeid
Robin Arculus
Alexi Arlidge
John Arpel
Keith Arundale
Michael Ashton
Commodore Martin Atherton OBE
Allan Douglas Atkinson
Ian Attwood
Austin Lewis Limited
Mark Avison
Kenneth Ayers MBE
Philippa Foster Back CBE
Paul Keith Bailey
Keith Baker
Captain Peter Baker RD DL RNR
Clive Bannister
John Barradell OBE
Deputy Doug Barrow
David Barzilay
David F. Batchelor
Commander R. M. H. Bawtree OBE
    RN
Richard C. Beale
Alderman Sir Michael and Lady Bear
Joan Beavington

Linda Bee
Robert Beecroft
Professor Trevor Beedham
Peter Beesley
Antonia D. Belcher
Ian Andrew Bellinger
Soheila Benlevi
Rod and Liz Bennion
Sir Christopher Benson
David Bentata
Professor R. J. Berry
Paul Bessemer
Sara Beswick
Mark Blandford-Baker
Geoffrey G. T. Blanford
Matt Bolton
Maureen Bonanno-Smith
Heyrick Bond-Gunning
S. A. C. Bonnington
Ernest Bounds
Gram Brazier
Jason Brazier
Kitty Brazier
Roy M. Brennan
The Worshipful Company
    of Brewers
Commodore Richard Bridges
Derek, Hilary, Heather and
    Thomas Briggs
Frances Broadway
Edward Brooke-Hitching
Emma Brooke-Hitching
Georgia Brooke-Hitching
Matthew Brooke-Hitching
William Brooke-Hitching
C. J. Brown
Colonel E. G. Brown
R. F. G. Brown
Rodney Gerard Brown
Neil Bruce-Copp OBE

Major General David Burden CB
    CVO CBE
John Burke
Peter and Anthea Burke
Anthony Burrell
Alistair Burrow
Matthew Burrow
Alison Burstall
James Burstall
Teresa Cahill
Nicholas Cambridge
Andy Cameron
Owen Campbell
P. A. Campfield
Lee Canderton
William Card
Jane Carey-Harris
The Worshipful Company
    of Carpenters
Stephen P. Carroll
Alisa Rebbeck Carter
Sir John Chalstrey
Judith Chandler
John Chapman
John D. Chapman
The Charles Family
Norman Christy
Lieutenant Colonel W. J. H. Clark
Graham Clarke
Peter Clarke
William Donald Cleaver
Commander James Cohen RD RNR
Michael Cohen
Nicola Cohen
Sub Lieutenant Oliver Cohen RNR
Jill Conby
Barbara Connell
Eileen Connell
Dr C. K. Connolly TD
Carlo Consolante

Paul Constantinidi
The Cook and The Butler Event Company
Lieutenant Commander D. J. Cooper
    RD RNR
Lucy June Cooper
Ian Cordingley
Richard Cory-Pearce
Dan Craig
Hermione Crosfield
Alistair Bassett Cross
Edward Crouch
Peter Crouch
Major General Sir William Cubitt
    KCVO CBE
Michael Cumper
Andrew Cuthbert
Karen Da Silva
John Dallimore
Peter Dart
Edward Norman David
Colin and Roberta Davies
Martin J. Davies
Andrew Daw
Master Leonardo Dimaguila
Michelle Dite
David J. Double
Deputy Billy Dove OBE
The Drapers' Company
Michael St G. N. Drewitt
Tony Drewitt
Roger Duckworth
Frederick J. Dudley
John Lee Dumbrell
Hew R. Dundas
The Dunloy Accordian Band
Sally Dymott
Oliver Eccles
Theo Eccles
Matthew Edwards
Michael Edwards

Geoffrey Ellis
Philip Ellson
Graham Elms
Peter H. English MBE
Alderman Peter Estlin
Lieutenant Colonel Claire Evans TD
Gerry Everett
Lieutenant Colonel Brian Fahy MBE
The Worshipful Company of
    Fan Makers
David Farrington
Alan Felt
J. J. Fenwick
James Fforde
Edward Field
Helen Field
Hugh Oliver Field
Mark Field
Midshipman Maxim Field RNR
Tom and Win Field
David A. E. Finch
The Fishmongers' Company
Colin Fleming
William Forrester
Rodney Foster
C. R. S. Fowler TD DL
Sir William Francis CBE
A. R. G. Frase
William B. Fraser
Anthony and Elisa Gabb
William Gardiner
Gerald A. Garnett
A. C. S. Gibbs
Paul Vincent Gifford
Colonel Nigel Gilbert
Girlguiding London and
    South East England
Julie Gladwin
The Worshipful Company of Glaziers
    and Painters of Glass
Michael Godbee
Chris Godbold
Colonel Geoffrey Godbold OBE TD
    DL
Richard S. Goddard
Dr John Goldsworth
Evadne Gordon
Chris Gotch
Janet P. Gotch
Trevor Gould
Mark Gower-Smith
Alderman Alison Gowman
Michael S. K. Grant

Arthur and Susan Gray
Anthony Richard Withers Green
Douglas James Green
Trevor Green
The Grocers' Company
Loyd Grossman
Rudolf Grotefels
Leslie Grout
James Gurling
John M. Guttridge
The Haberdashers' Company
David Hadden
Alderman Timothy Hailes JP
Major Christopher R. Hall TD
Peter Hall
Andrew Halle
Anna Gieskens Hallett
In Memory of Sue Hammerson CBE
Ted Hannon
Nigel Harding
Lieutenant Commander Richmal
    Hardinge RNR
Mark and Mary Hardy
Michael Harrison
Anthony J. Hart OBE DSC JP
Colin A. Hart JP
Warren Haskins
Colonel Mark Hatt-Cook OBE RD*
Christopher Hayman
Trevor Haynes
The Reverend John Hayton
Paul R. Heasmer
Dr and Mrs T. A. Heathcote
Volker G. Heinz
Colin Hellyer
Stephen Henderson
Michael Henderson-Begg MBE
Paul Herbage MBE
Commander John Herriman RNR
Professor Joe L. and
    Helene R. Herzberg
Jean Hewitt
Linseyanne Hewitt
Martin J. Hewitt
Alderman Peter Hewitt
John Hickman
Roy Hidson
Sydney A. J. Hill
Edward Hoefling
Raymond Hofmann
Nigel Hollebone
Sir David Howard Bt
Peter and Lin Hughes

Lesley Ann Hunt
John and Brenda Hurn
Jack D. Imos
Walter Isler
Judith Anne Jackson
Commander Rory Jackson RN
David George Jagger
Paul D. Jagger
Brian James
Michael James
Gemma Jamieson
Karl Jarvis
Diana I. Jervis-Read
The Jimmy Mizen Foundation
Victoria Johns
Archer Jones
Glyn Edward Jones
Lou Jones
Matilda Jones
Michael Jones
Melina Joy
Patrick R. Joyce
Norman Kaphan
Keele University
Michael J. Kelly
Angus Kennedy
Nicholas Stuart Kerr
Joan Doris Kertland
Stephen Kibbey
Robin King
Kingston and Malden Scout
    and Guide Band
Alexander Kramarenko
Edmund Kruszelnicki
Joy F. Laister
Nicholas K. Laister
Brian Lamden
Terence Robert Last
Zoe Laver
Andrew Lavis
Carol Lazarus
Anthony Le Cras
Christine Lea
The Leathersellers' Company
David and Vivienne Lester
Lord Levene
Mrs A. Levison
Peter Lisley
J. F. Livingston
D. Lloyd
Morag Loader
John Lockyer
Peter Logsdon

London Metropolitan University
Deborah Long
Robin Long
Lieutenant Colonel I. D. Lonsdale
Bob Lovell
Archie Lovelock
Lily-Mae Lovelock
J. W. N. Lowes
Brian Lowing
Jan Lowy
Barry Lucas
Alderman Ian Luder
Lin Luder
Commander John Ludgate RD* DL
    RNR
Peter E. Lumley
George MacLean
Lieutenant Commander Nicholas P.
    Maclean RD RNR
Alan Maidment
Conor Maile
Kathryn Maile
Rae Maile
Peter Mantell TD
The Mason Family
The Honourable Company of
    Master Mariners
Brian Matthews
C. W. and C. E. Maude
Richard Maxey
Hamish McArthur
Peter McCafferty
Paul McCracken
Amy McKee
Colonel Ian W. B. McRobbie OBE
    TD DL
Richard D. W. Mead
Wendy Mead OBE CC
Karl Meade
Robin Meech
David I. Meggitt
Brian Edward Meredith
Montague J. Meyer
Charles Miller
Elizabeth Mills OBE
Lyn Mills
Chris Monk
Giles Morgan
Fran Morrison
The Very Reverend Dr John Moses
Carl Moss
Father Derek Mottershead
Margot E. Mouat

Alderman the Lord Mountevans
and Lady Mountevans
Adrian Mumford
Don Munro
Colonel R. W. Murfin TD DL
David Murgatroyd
Lucy Musgrave
Muhsin Mustafa
S. E. T. Neale
Donald and Rosemary Newell
Derek J. Newton
Canon Nigel Nicholson DL
James Nisbet
Captain Chris Norman
James North
J. R. L. (Bob) Nuttall
Brian Nuttell
Jonathan O'Brien
Antony R. O'Hagan
Dr Peadar O'Mórdha
Squadron Leader Kevin
O'Shaughnessy
John Oakley-Smith JP
Andreas Oertli
Adrian Oliver
Sir Michael Oliver
Tim Oliver
David Philip Olliver
Erik Alan Olliver
The Opcyon Design Company
Limited
Clive Osborne
Wing Commander Chris Owen AE
John Palloway
Ric and Jenette Parker
Alderman and Sheriff Dr Andrew
Parmley
Rita Pattinson
Mrs P. Pearce
Peter and Angela Pelosi and Family
Tristan B. Peniston-Bird
Elizabeth Perree
Paul Anthony Phillips
Anthony Philpott
Helen Pickstock
The Worshipful Company
of Plaisterers
The Worshipful Company of Makers
of Playing Cards
Owen, Jacqui, Jemma and
Lauren Pocock
Major Alison Price
Simon Probert

Jeff Protheroe
Nigel Pullman
Dr Michael Purshouse
Alan and Pennie Radcliffe
Megan Radcliffe
Christopher B. Ratcliffe
Leslie Reason
Alderman Neil Redcliffe
Eugene Regan
Dominic Reid OBE
Elizabeth Reid
Grace Reid
James Reid
Suzannah Reid
Suzanne Reid
Sylvia Reid
Tony and Penny Reid
Lois Reynolds
Judith Rich OBE
Clive Richards OBE DL
J. A. Ridge
John Ridgeway
Murray Roberts
Timothy J. Roberts
Alex Robertson
Baron Robertson of Ormond
Francine Roccia
John Roper
Royal Society of St George, City
of London Branch
Chris Ruff
Ian Russell
The Saddlers' Company
Major Alex Saunders
Lieutenant Commander Tony Scott
RNR
Martin Secrett
Belinda and Michael Selley-Tregear
Major R. J. Seargent
Colin Sewell-Rutter
Eric Shawyer
Penelope Shelley MBE
Vickie Sheriff
Michael Simmonds
Raymond John Simpson
Stephen D. and Linda A. Simpson
Emily Skinner
Edward Slade
Derek Smedley
Catherine Smith
Graeme M. Smith CC
Linda J. Smith JP
Brian Sole

Graham C. Somerville
Roger Southam
The Worshipful Company of
Spectacle Makers
Duncan Spence
H. W. Spicer TD
Spitalfields City Farm
Jackie Springett
Richard Springford
Andrew Spurling
G. B. Standring
The Worshipful Company of
Stationers and Newspaper Makers
Malcolm Stephen
K. D. Stern
Patrick Streeter
Wendy Stringer
Richard and Lolyn Sutton
Clare Sweatman
Paul and Sharon Taberer
William, Jo, Georgina and
Hannah Tall
Judy Tayler-Smith
Melissa Taylor
Rodney and Janet Taylor
Peter Thompson
Deputy James M. D. Thomson
Rex Thornborough RD*
Richard Thorne
Adèle Thorpe
John G. Thorpe
Matthew S. W. Tilbury
Keith Torrance
Ian Wilson Tough JP
Maureen Townend
Melanie Trapnell
Major Sandy Tudor TD
Trevor W. Tupholme
Variety, The Children's Charity
Julian Verden
Sir Lawrence and Lady Zoe Verney
James A. Vickers
Mark Vickers
Victoria College Exams
Squadron Leader M. Vincenti MBE
Anthony Vlasto
Simon Wainwright
Lieutenant Colonel Edward G.
Waite-Roberts TD
Commander D. A. Wakefield RN
Constance and Ned Wakeman
Waldburg Shire Horse Team
Alexander H. E. D. Walduck

Nicholas S. R. D. Walduck
Richard and Susie Walduck
Rebecca Walker
Squadron Leader Graham Waller
The Company of Pikemen and
Musketeers, HAC
Lieutenant Commander Tim Ware
RD RNR
Olive Waring
Diane and Alan Warman
Raymond Warner BEM
The Worshipful Company of
Water Conservators
Ian R. S. Watson
Tim Watts
Major I. R. Weatherley
Lieutenant Commander John R.
Wesley RD RNR
Graham R. Westcott MBE
A. F. Wheeler
Mark Wheeler
John D. G. White
Ann Wickham
Pamela Gay Widmer
Jack Wigglesworth
Edward Wild
Professor Richard Wilding OBE
Colonel Dick Wilkinson TD
Eileen V. R. Williams
Elaine D. Williams
Jackie Williams
John H. J. Williams
Dr Keith C. Williams
Luke G. D. Williams
Joyce and Ken Willis
Jonathan Willmott
Lieutenant Colonel N. H.
Woellwarth
Colonel Andrew Charles Wood TD
Nicholas Wood
Simon C. Wood
Peter and Lesley Woodward
Charles Peter Wraith
C. G. S. and R. E. Wynterbee-Robey
John D. Yates
Gregory Young
135 Geographic Squadron RE

· INDEX ·

·ACKNOWLEDGMENTS

pp.2–3 © Museum of London/The City of London Corporation; pp.6–7 Finn Bruce/FCB Productions; p.8 Private collection of Dominic Reid; p.10 The Fishmongers' Company; p.11 Private collection of Dominic Reid; pp.12–13 © City of London; p.13 George Ramsay; p.14 © Imperial War Museum (Q 69032); p.15 Private collection of Dominic Reid; pp.16–17 © Museum of London; pp.18–19 George Ramsay; p.20 The National Archives, Kew, ref. E 42/79; p.21 © City of London; p.22 London Metropolitan Archives, City of London; p.23 Ben Stansall/AFP/Getty Images & London Metropolitan Archives, City of London; pp.24–25 © The British Library Board. Maps.Crace.Port.1.33; p.25 Heritage Image Partnership Ltd/Alamy; pp.26–27 RIBA Collections; pp.28–29 George Ramsay; p.30 Rod Williams/Alamy (t), © Museum of London (b); p.31 © Guildhall Art Gallery, City of London; p.32 Julian Woodford; p.33 © City of London (t), © Illustrated London News Ltd/Mary Evans (b); p.36 Carl Impey (l & r); p.37 Private collection of Dominic Reid (t), Carl Impey (b); p.38 akg-images/Florilegius; pp.38–39 VIEW Pictures Ltd/Alamy; p.40 & p.41 The Worshipful Company of Pattenmakers; p.42 & p.43 Museum of the Order of St John, London; p.44 Christ's Hospital School (t), Malcolm Park editorial/Alamy (b); p.45 © City of London (t), Christ's Hospital School (b); pp.46–47 Private collection of Dominic Reid; p.48 The National Archives, Kew; p.49 akg-images/Imagno (t), © Clive Totman (b); p.50 © Richard Davies; pp.50–51 © Clive Totman; p.52 Bishopsgate Library, Bishopsgate Foundation and Institute; p.53 Private collection of Dominic Reid (t), Harald Joergens (b); p.54 © Sotheby's/akg-images; p.55 © City of London (t), Carl Court/Getty Images (b); pp.56–57 George Ramsay; p.58 © Dean and Chapter of Westminster/John McEwan; p.59 Courtesy of Saint Bartholomew's Hospital Archives (SBHB/HC/1/1550)/John McEwan; pp.60–61 College of Arms MS M11 fo. 21v and 22, © College of Arms; p.62 © The Trustees of the British Museum; p.63 George Ramsay (l), © Museum of London/Henry Grant Collection (r); p.64 Guildhall Library & Art Gallery/Heritage Images/Getty Images (t), © Museum of London (b); p.65 Malcolm Knight; p.66 Oxford University Press; p.67 Private collection of Dominic Reid (t), George Ramsay (b); p.68 akg-images/Imagno/Austrian Archives (S) (l), George Ramsay (r); p.69 © Guildhall Art Gallery, City of London (t), Suzanne Plunkett/Reuters/Corbis (b); p.70 & p.71 George Ramsay; p.72 © City of London; p.73 Daniel Greenhouse/Alamy (l), Ghent University Library (r); p.74 © The British Library Board. Add. 28330 f.30; p.75 George Ramsay; p.76 George Ramsay (all); p.77 The Art Archive/David Boyer/NGS Image Collection; pp.78–79 London Metropolitan Archives, City of London/Bridgeman Images; p.80 Classic Image/Alamy; p.81 © The British Library Board. Royal 18 E. I f.172 (det); pp.82–83 © The British Library Board. Royal 18 E. I, f.175; p.83 Bedfordshire and Luton Archives and Records Service, BOR B/A1/6; p.84 akg-images/Archie Miles; pp.84–85 Mary Evans Picture Library; p.85 The Art Archive/John Meek; p.86 Utrecht University Library, MS. 1196 fo. 49v; p.87 Utrecht University Library, MS. 1196 fo. 50v (l), © National Portrait Gallery, London (r); p.88 PjrTravel/Alamy; p.89 Guildhall Library, City of London; p.90 © National Portrait Gallery, London (l), © Worshipful Company of Ironmongers (r); p.91 © Illustrated London News Ltd/Mary Evans; p.92 The Fishmongers' Company (l & r); pp.92–93 The Fishmongers' Company; p.93 Royal Collection Trust/© Her Majesty Queen Elizabeth II 2014; p.95 © Guildhall Art Gallery, City of London; pp.96–97 © Museum of London/Bridgeman Images; p.98 & p.99 © City of London; p.100 © Imperial War Museum (Q 54603) (tr), © Imperial War Museum (Q 85980) (bl); p.101 © Illustrated London News Ltd/Mary Evans; p.102 Galerie Bilderwelt/Bridgeman Images (background), © Illustrated London News Ltd/Mary Evans (inset); p.103 © Illustrated London News Ltd/Mary Evans (t & b); pp.104–105 Gaumont British Picture Corporation/ITV Studios Global Entertainment; p.106, p.107 & pp.108–109 Yale Center for British Art; pp.110–111 London Metropolitan Archives, City of London; pp.112–113 Private collection of Dominic Reid; p.115 & pp.116–117 © Guildhall Art Gallery, City of London; p.118 The Goldsmiths' Company; p.120 © The Trustees of the British Museum; p.121 © The Trustees of the British Museum; p.122 © Illustrated London News Ltd/Mary Evans; p.123 *The Illustrated London News*; p.124 Gaumont British Picture Corporation/ITV Studios Global Entertainment; pp.124–125 British Film Institute; p.125 Gaumont British Picture Corporation/ITV Studios Global Entertainment; p.126 Showcase Presents Dr. No (#43), published by DC Comics/National Periodical Publications, 1963, from comicsagogo.com; p.127 Danjaq/Eon/UA/The Kobal Collection; pp.128–129 Artwork © John Burningham. Published by arrangement with Random House Children's Publishers UK, a division of The Random House Group Limited; p.130 Private collection of Dominic Reid; pp.130–131 The Postal Museum, formerly the British Postal Museum & Archive; p.131 Private collection of Dominic Reid; pp.132–133 © Illustrated London News Ltd/Mary Evans.

Front cover and endpapers: © Sir Peter Blake 2015. Original artwork specially commissioned to celebrate the 800th anniversary of the Lord Mayor's Show.

Back cover: George Ramsay (top left & right); © Guildhall Art Gallery, City of London (bottom left); The Fishmongers' Company (bottom right).

Every effort has been made to contact the copyright owners of all images featured in this book. In the case of an inadvertent omission, please contact Third Millennium Publishing, 3 Holford Yard, Bevin Way, London WC1X 9HD, United Kingdom.

The Doves Type is an updated digital facsimile of the iconic type used by the Doves Press in the early 20th century. Small quantities of the original metal type were recovered from the Thames in 2014. Recreated by Robert Green, it is available from www.typespec.co.uk.

'Watching the Show' by the Gentle Author was first published online on 15 November 2010 at www.spitalfieldslife.com, under the title 'At the Lord Mayor's Show'.

Route map on pp.34–35 drawn and illustrated by Kevin Freeborn, based on Open Street Map; © Open Street Map contributors.

First published in Great Britain in 2015 by Third Millennium Publishing,
an imprint of Profile Books Ltd

3 Holford Yard
Bevin Way
London WC1X 9HD
United Kingdom
www.tmiltd.com

A CIP catalogue record for this book is available from The British Library.

ISBN: 978 1 908990 55 6
e-ISBN: 978 1 782832 75 1

General Editor: Dominic Reid
Editor and project manager: Hannah Bowen
Design: Matthew Wilson
Production: Debbie Wayment

Reprographics by Tag Publishing, London
Printed and bound in Italy by Printer Trento srl
on acid-free paper from sustainable forestry